KINGSWAY

REMEMBERING THE PAST, DEFINING THE
FUTURE

CHRISTOPHER R. KING

33ink
PUBLISHING

33ink, Inc. a Cruzach, Inc. Company
9663 Santa Monica Boulevard, Suite 363
Beverly Hills, CA 90210
www.33ink.com

Printed in the United States of America

10 9 8 7 6 5 4 3 2 1

First edition 2020

Photos by Meeno
Art direction by Christopher R. King
Front & back cover design by David Schwartz

Library of Congress Cataloging-in-Publication Date is available

ISBN 978-1-7349555-2-1 (paperback)
ISBN 978-1-7349555-1-4 (ebook)

DEDICATION

Thank you, God for your mercy and grace in my life, for all things are possible with you.

To my mother Karen, my sister Leah, and my grandmother Jean, three strong women who raised me: You have always had my back and always stood by me even in the worst of times.

To my sons, Cruz and Zachary, I am so proud of the little men you are becoming. You have taught me so many great things about life, myself and unconditional love since your birth. I hope I always make you proud and may you understand more about your life and your calling as you are older. Daddy loves you so much!

To my business partner and dear friend Rob Dyrdek, you believed and pushed me to fulfill my calling! I am forever grateful. To all my other business partners, my friends who are like family, and all who have supported me since day one, thank you. I couldn't have done it without you.

INTRODUCTION

Real-life lessons from Christopher R. King

This book is a blueprint for success. Christopher R. King has made and lost fortunes with a variety of industries, and through a lifetime of sometimes painful lessons, he offers his take on what it is to be an entrepreneur. This is an honest, and at times, blunt essay chronicling his journey to realize his dreams. A relentless man on a mission, his aim is to help you realize your full potential.

CONTENTS

FOREWORD

By Kenny Kemp

I remember the very first time meeting Christopher R. King. Among the first things you notice about him is that he is neat, scrupulously so. Sure, he loves to wear fine and expensive clothing and display the ornamentation of wealth. He is fastidious and likes order and tidiness. His philosophy? A place for everything and everything in its place. His collection of beautiful cars are well-polished and gleaming every day; his office is scrubbed and tidy; his Beverly Hills home is in order, tranquil, and pin-clean. Peering in his closet, his shirts, his shoes, his suits, and his pants are all meticulously clean and pressed, and lined up on racks, even color-coded on expensive wooden hangers. Winter attire is stored in wardrobes or in Louis Vuitton boxes and hand-made hard case trunks. His living room shelves are neat, bookshop-straight rows of his favorite and most inspiring books, a sign of his on-going thirst for learning. His expansive open-plan kitchen, which is not for show, but where he cooks regularly, is pristine with every utensil polished and tucked away in its place.

He is exceptionally well-groomed, right down to his polished nails and his monogrammed, silk foulard pochette. His style doesn't stop with formal dress, and even while dressing down casually in Brunello Cucinelli pants, Tom Ford loafers, and an untucked Brioni monogrammed dress shirt, he remains impeccable. As with everything else Mr. King does, everything is thoughtfully considered.

All of this fastidious precision suggests an individual who has pulled himself through the grime, the grunge, and the grit of life to reach his goals. He has made a choice: he prefers the golden glow of good-living to a gravel-dirt view of simply "getting by." It also suggests he has a tidy mind too – which has given him the ability to clear out any extraneous and lingering negativity and retaining a positive mindset that has given him such a varied and interesting life. In my thirty years as an international journalist and human observer, Christopher King ranks in the top echelon of similarly accomplished, intriguing, and multi-faceted gentlemen.

Moreover, the world desperately needs people like Mr. King. He is a phenomenon. He is a doer who does not hang around moping. If the energy in the room shifts and becomes unduly negative, I've witnessed him walk out and find a way to recharge his battery. He is his own breed. A one of a kind even. It can be a whirlwind of experiences spending time with him. Yet, he can be quiet, reflective, and yes, vulnerable too. Others who have taken the kind of punches and knocks, both mental and physical, that have rained down on Christopher King would curl up and cower in a corner. Yet he licks his wounds and gets back in the game. He is the personification of the revived American Dream in the age of post-truth cynicism, relentless social media, and high-definition celebrity. He is influential, yet he is not a massive household name. I could add, *yet*. He is a role model – and that makes him worth observing.

He built one empire in real estate in Atlanta, lost it in the great financial crash of 2008, and he brushed off the dust and dirt of defeat. Since then, he has been able to build other multi-million dollar ventures based in Beverly Hills. So far, that's pretty damn impressive for an aggressive youth who dropped out of a Connecticut high school after a brawl. He ended up learning his early adult lessons about life on the streets, riding a pallet in a warehouse jungle, and setting up a landscaping business at seventeen. In our conversations, he is candid about so many aspects of his life. He admits to making glaring mistakes, and he is repentant. "I've changed as a human being to evolve and become successful in life. It's why I'm here today living my dream," he says.

Critics say he is brash, self-centered, and even flashy. Yet somehow this narcissistic stereotype doesn't fit Christopher R. King. He does care: he is genuinely concerned about others, and he shares his success in a generous way. He can also be tough, unflinching and intimidatingly blunt, which can be essential attributes for doing business and making money. I have seen how he lights up a room and exudes warmth. Those who know him best – his long-term friends and loyal work colleagues – describe him as generous, humorous, driven, passionate, inclusive, and inspirational.

Today he has teamed up with another self-made, successful entrepreneur, Rob Dyrdek, familiar across the US for his prowess as a professional skateboarder, and the host of a variety of reality television programs, but less well-known as a successful private equity investor with a network of businesses. Dyrdek describes King as a long-lost brother who shares a similar working-class background, coupled with a raw determination to succeed. Dyrdek and King started working in tandem and are developing a unique luxury company destined to become influential. That's his crystal-clear goal. You certainly wouldn't want to bet against this.

PREFACE

By Christopher R. King

I originally had the idea to write a book back in 2013. I remember my publicist and I thought it would be a good idea to start this process, and we started interviewing authors from around the world. I was in Miami that day, and I had just checked into the St. Regis in Bal Harbor when my phone rang with a call from my assistant who had both my publicist and Kenny Kemp on the phone. Kenny wrote the book *Business Stripped Bare* with Richard Branson. We had a deep conversation, and therefore he was at the top of our list. After a few more phone calls and an email with a personal recommendation from Sir Richard himself, I knew he was the right man for the job, and we quickly began to work. I flew him in from Scotland, and we started a rather involved process that lasted almost a year. I have a confession, I really never wanted to write a book. I felt I hadn't done anything worth filling the pages of a book. I still felt that what most people viewed as big milestones or successes weren't quite enough for me.

In one of our first conversations, I asked Kenny: *What are we doing? Who would even read a book about my life?* It was because of that hesitation and uncertainty as to whether or not the book would be well-regarded that I shelved it. This was a process that I started and stopped a few times over the years.

However, it wasn't until Rob Dyrdek and I started building our luxury brand that I began to consider writing again. And this was only because I told him about the book. In typical Dyrdek fashion, he insisted I send it to him. He read the first draft and said, "You've got to finish this and put it out." Still, I felt the hesitation, but with his energy and belief in the project, we immediately jumped back in. I flew Kenny Kemp back out to Beverly Hills and got him rewriting and tweaking the book – only to shelf it again, I felt it wasn't the right time.

You see, for me this isn't a biography and this is not my entire story. These are just bits and pieces of my life, which have helped to shape much of the man that I am today. It wasn't until the global Coronavirus crisis occurred that I was left wondering what could I do while being home and wanting to work.

One of the things that most people who are close to me admire is that I've never been afraid to fail! I had to pick myself back up from ground zero many times. With everything that's going on in the world right now, we are going to have to collectively, as an entire human race, find ways to start over or make changes.

I do view myself to be this courageous, persistent, and resilient machine with a relentless work ethic. I do not however, view myself as this massive success story. I always do though find a way to come out of whatever life throws at me with a smile. There is never going to be a better time to put this book out. This is a time when the world is home practicing quarantine while this virus passes. People are uncertain, nervous, and will surely want a positive perspective on how to start over.

It was like a bolt of lightning went off in my body. I became a man on a mission, re-reading, getting back in touch with all the contributors, revisiting, and reworking to offer this first book.

I've been through so much over the past three years. What better time to give hope and encouragement stemming from real-life stories of failure and success?

I pray that whoever reads this book understands: You're never alone, and we all have more failures than we care to admit. It is my hope that you find parts of this book encouraging, motivational, and inspiring, and I hope that these words get you up, get you out, and get you going back at life again.

SECTION I: THE SETUP

I. THE BEGINNING

Let me introduce myself properly. My name is Christopher R. King. I am an American entrepreneur, visionary, and designer living in Beverly Hills. My work takes me around the globe, often to new places. I love the experience of travel, meeting a number of different people with their own skills and passions, and discovering more about their world. They say that travel broadens the mind. This has been true for me, because I've seen with my own eyes how the finer things in life are created; I've tasted some of the most exquisite food and wine, produced by artisans who are deeply zealous about what they make.

My quest and the aspiration to find the very best continues to strongly influence me, while defining my direction both in life and in business. It's what I call the Kingsway!

I was a high school dropout who quit school in the tenth grade and became a multi-millionaire, not once but twice. While I don't have regrets, I learned the hard way. I think that my life experiences have helped me get to where I am right now. It is a deeply personal story that I would like to share with you in this book. From the beginning, I told my mother I would go further with my GED than any of the people in my class who had made it with their high school diploma. I feel I have done that. Maybe having a collection of degrees would have made it easier on me, that just wasn't my journey. In fact, at age twelve, I became aware that I was destined to be different. Greatness was calling me, though I didn't yet know what it would look like.

Now, I am not here to advocate whether or not school is for you, taking the conventional road to success is smart for most who have aspirations to attend college or university. However, it wasn't my path. The college path should never be viewed as the *only* way to make it in life. I hope by me sharing my story, it will inspire those who have fallen, those who have had to start over. In my book, there are two types of people: Those who have failed so many times that they may feel that there isn't a way out, and those who have faced adversity and learned the hard way. There are too many people in the world today who are afraid to try. Too many people have been knocked down and have had a hard time getting back up. I have heard people say that switching gears or reinventing yourself in life is one of the hardest things you can do. I know people get stuck when things get tough, and some even give up. Some are so discouraged that they don't even think about trying again. I didn't have any other choice. I had big dreams. I have had to evolve and reinvent myself over and over again. You know what I've discovered? I actually enjoy it.

While I have been faced with several major setbacks over the years, I knew that there was something inside me that seemed to relish the rebuilding process, the "give-it-all-you-got" mentality that pushes you to rebound from rock bottom back to the top. I could almost sense the rush of endorphins pumping into my brain. I love the hustle and anticipation and the satisfaction of a comeback. As our cells break down and new ones come along, regeneration is a vital aspect of the human existence. So why not have the same thing happen with what we do? It must be ingrained in my DNA that I want to prove that I can do it. I have done this time and time again.

I'm thankful for a life of "hard knocks." There is also something to be said about figuring it out on your own. I have taken advantage of the unique perspective from coming out of nothing. Not because I wanted to, but because there was no other way for me to rise to the top. I have seen how the world works first-hand coming from nothing and achieving something. It was these humble beginnings that kept me grounded and acted as the fuel I needed on my way to the top.

I am here to tell you that everything and anything is possible. I have experienced life to the fullest. You shouldn't accept or listen to anyone who tells you it isn't possible, because it is possible. If you feel you've been knocked down, written-off by your upbringing, are facing tough problems, and feel like you will never achieve your dreams, I hope you find meaningful messages in my story to help you find your way.

How can I write a book about all this? After all, I'm just a kid who hustled and worked hard every single day of my life. I was a teenager growing up in tough neighborhoods in the 1990s. My adolescent eclectic soundtrack was made of Wu Tang Clan, A Tribe Called Quest, Frank Sinatra, Guns N' Roses, Stevie Wonder, and James Brown. Downtown Hartford, Connecticut was a violent place, and I became immersed in the alternative urban sound, style, and culture. Then, long before the explosion of mobile apps and social media, I learned how to hustle. This was all before inspirational master classes, YouTube tutorials, or Instagram influencers were on the scene. I had no choice but to find my own path and fight for it.

As I was encouraged by friends to tell my story, I thought, *What could I say that might make a difference to anyone reading this? Who the hell is going to read a book about my life lessons anyway?* I mean, *Who was I? What did I do that was so great?* Sure, there were plenty of things I could say, yet not said before by others – and often more eloquently? But through many conversations, I was reassured that my story was unique and that I should share it. It was suggested that I should give people insight into my mindset and show them the tools and attitude that helped me make something out of my life. I went from nothing not once but twice! More important than the money or accolades, the same insight has helped me find peace, happiness, and true joy in life, even during some of the most difficult of times.

I had several brainstorming sessions to lock down what to say, how to say it, what was important, and what wasn't. Of course, there are many stories from my life and situations that didn't make this book. I wanted to focus on the most meaningful stories that might inspire someone.

Let me tell you what this is *not*. This is not my life story or an autobiography – that's for another time and place. This is a curated collection from my personal experiences. Along the way, I've been growing and learning about love, faith, fatherhood, friendship, patience, wisdom, and the true meaning of life. I've picked up a lot along the way. No matter what your current situation in life is, background, upbringing or your experience, hopefully you will gain some knowledge in this book that you can apply to your life.

This book is an honest look at what I've learned, and how I used this practical knowledge to follow my dreams. The same outcome can happen for you. Nothing is impossible!

II. GET YOUR HEAD IN THE GAME

Over the last twenty years, I have built over a dozen businesses, some successful while others, well … they became my life lessons. From the outside looking in, it would be easy to think that money is my main driving force, but it's not. I've never been driven strictly by money. However, let's be honest for a second, having money in the bank enables you to do the things you want. It was always about the freedom to not let money make my choices for me; I never wanted my desires or dreams to stop because I didn't have the means to pursue them. So, in a way, it is about the freedom of choice. Once I established that philosophy, and stopped chasing the checks and started chasing good business with great people, I was able to really get into my flow.

Yet my story wasn't a straight shot. I was expelled from high school after a brawl with a bully, defending a younger classmate. I have always believed in standing up for what you believe in, but this singular event ended up being one of my earliest defining moments (some would say a mistake, let's call this a "life lesson"). From that moment on, I did what it took to survive. I worked as a dishwasher and a line cook in local restaurants. I cut grass and

trimmed hedges as a landscaper. I even drove a pallet-jack in a sub-zero warehouse jungle. Before I was twenty-five, I wore a bullet-proof vest during some of my crazy days as a hip-hop promoter which eventually led to owning my nightclub. Later I moved to Atlanta, Georgia to take a stab at real estate. It's here that I rebuilt a beat-down home in less than forty-five days with my own sweat equity and flipped it for a $65,000 profit.

I grew up learning life the hard way and over time, I began to have faith in my abilities and myself early on. I formed a belief that I could do anything if I focused my mind to it, a lesson I keep close to my heart to this day. I believe that you can do whatever you want as long as you are willing to learn, be open-minded, and work your tail off!

Show Them You Belong

It was around 2006, I was in Miami on my way to an exclusive party with Patrick T. Cooper, who was a globally well-known wardrobe stylist. The thing was, we weren't invited. We were dressed to the nines, and as we stepped out of the limo, he looked me over as he buttoned his Armani suit. "If you know you belong here, they'll know you belong here as well! Now follow me and do as I do," he instructed.

We strode out towards the entrance, he had such confidence, because he knew that we would get in. We belonged. Simple as that. I have never in my life seen a security guard move so quickly to open a door. With our heads up, we walked past the party hostess with her phone, clipboard, and her earpiece. She didn't even ask our names or for our IDs. We were waved in. This is a lesson that still holds true today. I knew then that if I wanted to go somewhere in life, I first had to have the confidence to *know* where I was going. Then I had to visualize already being there. After that, it was simply an exercise in acting and knowing that I belonged. Visualization is a strong tool and one of the key components in life. It has played a major part in mine. I believe that I am the

creator of my destiny based on these beliefs, no matter the situation.

This is how I've been able to catapult myself to where I am now. I care passionately about seeing my ideas come to fruition, which extends to the growth and development of my employees, brands, and companies. I care about my children, family, and friends; I want them to excel in their lives too. I prefer not to dwell on the past, and I rarely look back. The lessons I have learned from growing up have all been about the empowerment of "doing it for yourself" – and believing in your own abilities. There is nothing you cannot do!

Subconsciously, I think that we often caution children not to reach for the stars or to follow their dreams because it might appear to be too hard or unrealistic, or maybe parents simply want to help their children avoid disappointment. Most of the population has been conditioned to believe that it's not possible. I don't agree with this. Anything is possible if you believe in yourself and work really hard at it, you will then obtain it. It might not seem possible, but in this book, I share stories that even in the most adverse times or at the lowest points in my life, I have kept my eye on what was important to me. I held onto my dreams, my desires, and my belief that I was going to change my life for the better.

This is about your *mindset*. Those who set their minds on prosperity have it. Those who think in terms of good health, have it. Conversely, those who dwell on sickness, end up sick; those who fear failure and poverty, end up miserable and yes, poor. It's the law of attraction (or at least, it is "my law"). It still shocks me that the importance of mindset and the "Laws of Attraction" are not something that are taught to everyone at an early age. This underlying truth is left for most of us to figure out on our own. Unfortunately, some people are told that they are not worth anything and they tend to believe it. Let me make a statement right here: The way you feel, the way you act, and even your attitude ultimately attracts what you get and become in life. This law of attraction works like a magnet. If you feel lonely, you are going to feel even lonelier. Sorry, but it's true! If you feel unhappy, you are going to be unhappy. It's like a downward spiral. Often it seems beyond your control, but in most cases, it isn't. *You can choose. Yes, I believe you can choose to be more content and have more control with the world around you. When you realize you have the power to change your perspective, the possibilities are endless.*

When I was just a kid, I remember writing myself a check from my personal checking account for a million dollars. I probably didn't even have but a few hundred dollars in my account. I put that check in my wallet, and I looked at it every day. It was about mindset and a manifestation that I would cash this check one day. In Carol S. Dweek's book, *Mindset: The New Psychology of Success*, she writes that there are two kinds of thinking: a fixed mindset and a growth mindset.[1] Someone with a fixed mindset will say: *I can't do that.* While those who have a growth mindset will say: *I can't do that ... yet.* If you are like me, you will say: *I can do it now, and I will do it now.* If you believe that you can't improve on things, then the logical position is that you will never even try. The human brain is made primarily of fatty gray tissue, but it behaves like a muscle. Like all muscles, the more you use and train it, the stronger it becomes. It needs to be flexed and properly trained to reach its maximum potential.

I want to give credit here to someone who opened my mind to this in a fundamental way. Many years ago, T. Harv Eker set up a health and exercise business, building it up to ten stores in only two and a half years. He sold the business to a Fortune 500 firm for $1.6 million. He began coaching people and had the great idea of creating the StreetSmart Business School for people just like me who had never been to college to study business and economics. I was heading off on vacation to Puerto Rico around 2004 and bought a pile of books at the airport. One was Eker's small book, *Secrets of the Millionaire Mind.*[2] I could not put it down. It became my own blueprint. I read it twice on vacation that week and within a year, it completely changed my mindset, and I became independently wealthy. Talk about mindset! I don't want to steal any of Eker's thunder, as he points out that we live in a mental, emotional, spiritual, physical, and material world. It is difficult to discern where one stops and another begins. Lack of money is a symptom. Poor health is a symptom. He says that money is a result. Health is a result. So, what is the root cause? According to Eker's wealth file, rich people manage their money well, poor people mismanage theirs. There are certain universal truths that are obvious, but they still need to be said and repeated: To increase your wealth, you either have to earn more or live on less.

It was clear to me from Eker's book, that if you don't like the way your life is going, try not complaining for two weeks. It made me laugh when he pointed out that complainers usually have a tough life and that they are living, breathing "crap magnets." His "Law of Attraction" meant that when you are complaining, you are attracting crap into your life. He set up a challenge: For the next seven days, don't complain, not just out loud but in your head as well, (which is more difficult than you might think) and see how drastically your life changes. This one piece of advice is a golden nugget, because blame, justification, and complaining are all sickness pills that alleviate the stress of failure. I've found that a lot of people don't understand that – yet it is such a powerful piece of advice.

I know having a positive mindset opens up your opportunities and expands your knowledge and performance in life. You might not have been the most successful in your classroom, but intelligence can be developed by effort and persistence as the neurons in your brain are stimulated and connected. For example, we understood this when sports heroes such as Michael Jordan and Kobe Bryant became legends in their field, because they enhanced their natural ability, through training and hard work. It was much more than their physical abilities; it was mostly about their attitude. Jazz icon, Miles Davis hit the nail right on the head when he spoke about his attitude towards music, "Anybody can play, the note is only twenty percent, the attitude of the mother****** who plays it is eighty percent."

My mindset began shifting to be far more positive during my

Atlanta days. Once, I was holding a board meeting at my real estate company and started to get frustrated. I told my team that the reason we were not closing more properties and not hitting construction deadlines was because they kept thinking there was a backup plan. I said, "You guys look at something and figure you will always have Plan A and Plan B. There's only Plan A for me. In your mind, you are already giving yourself a way out. I focus all of my energy and drive towards making Plan A happen."

By keeping your focus on what you really want, you start to visualize it – the same way you do if you want to walk into that high-profile event I mentioned earlier – and truly make it happen. People think it is luck. There is no such thing, it is about keeping your head in the game. Your mind is so powerful. When you keep a singular focus on what you want, you would be amazed at what you can accomplish.

Reading became my classroom, and as I continued to educate myself more through reading during this time, I discovered Paulo Coelho's inspirational work *The Alchemist*.[3] I've read and re-read many of the brilliant things that he has written, but I always return to my favorite of his sayings, "If you fall down seven times, you get up eight times." I've been knocked down a thousand times in life – but I've always found the inner strength to stand up again and face the world. I have been embarrassed, ridiculed, and worse, but it does not stop me from getting back up! Today, I know I am a success precisely because I changed my mindset, which allowed me to change my destiny. It instilled in me the courage to keep battling on. I am not pretending it was easy. There were many times that I wanted to give up and throw in the towel, but you must not lose hope or faith. You have to keep fighting. I hope I can encourage you to never give up and keep going, no matter what life throws at you.

We need to understand that there is life and death in the power of the tongue. It is our mind that controls that. If fact, our speech center in the brain controls all of our nerves. According to research, the brain has total control and authority over all the nerves in your body. This is why your mindset and the words you speak are so important. If you simply speak out loud and say, "I'm tired," then your nerves receive this message and prepare your whole body to become tired. This has been proven recently by science; however, my favorite teaching is usually in the Bible. James 3:2 says, "For we stumble in many things, if anyone does not stumble in word, he is a perfect man, able also to bridle the whole body."[4] The point is that we become what we say and think, which is why it is important to start with your mindset.

Learning to Let Go

Another important lesson is learning to let go. Throughout this book, I offer lessons of personal failures and the ability I've developed to change my mindset and pick myself back up. In order to do so, I think there is a key factor that most people don't or won't accept.

We all make mistakes. I've certainly made plenty. We all have inner doubts, fears, insecurities, and there are things that make us angry, resentful, and jealous. I know from my own experience, that having issues as a child or a teenager, can haunt you later on in life. It can make you question yourself, your ability, and your worth. I have also learned that forgiveness has been the tool that has allowed me to not live in bitterness; it has allowed me to be blessed in all areas of my life and to let go of the things that did not feed my spirit. I have learned that you cannot let the past or other peoples' opinions or words affect the way you want to live your life. You have to watch your own thoughts, choose your words wisely, "Be quick to listen, slow to speak, and slow to become angry."[5] You have to maintain a positive perspective. Instead of allowing negativity to weigh you down, you have to use it as fuel for your aspirations. I must be frank, it's not always easy and don't expect it to be. I used to be very impatient and emotional with business matters. I felt I had something to prove and would get disappointed taking things to heart. I had to come to terms with being vulnerable, and I realized that there was nothing wrong with it, and that allowed me to grow and mature. You cannot take things personally in life. You ultimately have to realize that no one is going to live your life, and people will regularly let you down. So, don't let anyone force you off the path you've chosen. Take control. I'm not a shrink, a psychoanalyst, or a therapist, nor would I claim to be. I can only explain how I see things, and how it has worked for me. I've learned firsthand the power of self-control and self-belief. Curbing your aggression, guilt, anger, fear, hatred, and resentment is central to your overall health and success.

III. YOUR PAST DOESN'T HAVE TO BE YOUR FUTURE

I believe that one of the greatest accomplishments in life is to understand that your past, no matter how unfortunate, doesn't dictate your future. Your current situation doesn't have to be the end of the story. There is always a chance for change and for you to not be defined by your past. I remember receiving a text from my mother on my fortieth birthday with well wishes. In a rather long message, she wanted to explain how proud she was of me. One of her comments that stood out the most was, "You have come to realize that your childhood and your past is not something to erase, but rather to embrace and cherish." So many stories come to mind, and I want to try and share a few that while not necessarily my proudest moments, were both emotional and hard lessons; ultimately, they were vital to me growing up.

I was an angry kid. I stressed my mother out. I was constantly fighting at school, and she couldn't quite deal with me or my anger. Perhaps it was the result of the frustration I felt over my parents splitting up, in addition to most issues facing teenagers.

I got expelled during my sophomore year, which occurred after defending a younger classmate. Sean was an easy target for bullies.

He lived close to my grandmother's house and was funny and a bit goofy. I was walking from class when Sean approached me. "I don't know what to do. I don't know Chris, you gotta help me." I told him to calm down. "What's going on?" There was a senior kid who was picking on him and threatening him. This was the typical bully stuff that happens in high school. I asked where he was and that I would go talk to him and ask him to stop.

I walked outside the lunch area and as I approached him, he got up and walked towards me. Sean was standing at a distance behind me. My goal was to just ask the bully to stop. As he was walking, I said, "Hey man, just leave this kid alone. Obviously, you can kick his butt, and he is much smaller than you." To my surprise, he replied in anger and said, "What are you gonna do about it if I don't?" Before I could even reply back, he took a big swing at me. I ducked and returned with a hard right hook. Blood splattered and kids were screaming. Fight! I felt the adrenaline and was so pissed that he had swung at me that I kept going – another right, a left, an uppercut. He stumbled back as I yelled, "You started this bro." He took another big swing, and I grabbed him, a quick knee to his face and it was over. He fell to the ground. And now security was escorting me to the principal's office, where I was detained and the cops were called.

It was bad. He had a shattered nose. Later on, I had to attend court, because the kid's family tried to sue the school. I was suspended for two weeks and my mother wasn't happy at all. It was a rough two weeks and though I was able to return to school, it was just different. People didn't talk much to me and everyone was acting weird. Soon enough, I got called in the principal's office. I was told bad news, "Chris I am so sorry, but we just can't have you attend this school anymore. Parents and kids are fearful. Your anger in this fight was really bad; you caused major damage to someone." Before she could finish her thought, I responded back, "I have never gotten into a fight here before, and he started it!" Her next statement didn't seem fair. "We have made a decision and the school board has agreed to expel you from not only this school, but every other public school in the district."

This was crazy … I was instantly moved into an alternative school. It was where all the other angry and disgruntled kids were sent to. When I arrived, the doors and iron windows were closed shut. It was rough. There were constant fights. It was as if I was put into a ring every day, defending myself on the basketball court and during lunchroom brawls. It was about four months of hell. I couldn't even learn or get any work done without fighting. I had had enough. I asked for a meeting with my principal and remember that day very clearly. I walked in, and I told him that I could not learn. I told him that I could not be in this environment anymore. I told him that all I had done was get into this one fight and because of that, I had been expelled from public schools. There were fights every day, because no one in here cared to do anything with their life. I said that I wanted to go back to public school and finish high school and if I couldn't return to my school, I would quit. He responded that I was expelled from all public schools, and that he couldn't do that. So, I left that day and quit school on the spot, never to return.

I did promise my mother that I would go further with my GED than anyone else would with a high school diploma. I remember you had to go sign up to get a textbook. It was about six weeks of courses while attending classes to help study for the exam. I walked out of the office, tossed my textbook into the trash, jumped in the car, and told my mother the exact date of the exam. I've always been really smart and got great grades when I applied myself and was focused. I was not going to waste another six weeks of my life, so I went ahead and got a job and started to work. The six weeks passed, and I showed up for my exam. I aced it! I did not have one incorrect answer and that was the extent of my public education, but let me tell you, it wasn't the end of my life lessons.

One of the hardest moments of my adolescence was checking into a small psychiatric facility named Elmcrest, located in Portland, Connecticut. After several months of therapy sessions, my therapist thought it was in my best interest to spend some time there to get my anger under control. My mother was running out of options to help me, and while I didn't want to, I agreed to go. Imagine the vibe in the facility, a few bullies together thrown together all in close proximity to other kids with similar issues as mine, some worse. I had to make the best of a very volatile and dangerous situation. When I finally got out, I was seventeen, with no support, no place to go, and no real aspirations. I did what most young men of similar backgrounds do; I hung out with the wrong crowd, made friends with shady characters, and got myself in real trouble. It all brought me to stare down the barrel of a gun.

As I was mentioning, I ended up hanging out with guys who I had no business being with. But at the time, I didn't know any better. I remember one of those incidents all too well. I headed to Tennessee with a guy in hopes of retrieving money owed to him, to this day I am not sure what I was thinking. We drove for over fifteen hours to get there and it was a giant waste of time. We stayed for a few days and ended up getting into a fight and I decided to leave. I grabbed my bag and headed to a pay phone at the gas station down the street. It happened all of a sudden. I remember the barrel of a gun being shoved right in my chest as he pulled back the hammer and asked me with a cold look to take off my necklace. My young life started flashing right before my eyes. I remember thinking: *How is this happening? Here I am, in the middle of Tennessee, away from my hometown, I'm being robbed at gunpoint!* This had never happened to me, even with all the violence that I had witnessed back in Hartford. Then they asked for all my money. I reached into my pocket to give him whatever cash I had. I thought that the transaction was done, however, he looked at me with this evil eye and raised the gun to my head. He proceeded to tell me that it is not good enough and that I should get in his car. I knew the moment I got in that car that things would get really bad; I might not come back from this. I don't know what possessed me at the time, but I made this split decision given that tensions were high, and I calmly told him that I wasn't doing that. I began to turn around as he shoved the gun against the back of my head. He yelled at me to get in the car once more. I repeated as loud as I could that I wasn't getting in the car. "I don't know who you are. I saw nothing." I then slowly began to walk away. Those few seconds felt like a few minutes. All I kept thinking was I'm about to have my brains blown away. It was over! I heard a car door slam and screeching tires as his car took off onto the highway. After gathering myself, I was eventually able to get back home. I realized that I was never going to put myself in that type of situation again. That day, I decided that I was going to make some drastic changes and that I was not going to let my past mistakes define my future.

Reinventing my Future

When I was a small boy, I would draw a lot. I would spend hours with pencils and felt-tip pens trying to sketch cartoon characters. Designing and creating were always natural passions for me. It was my favorite escape in a small house where the tension between my mother and father was high. In my bedroom, I had a colorful Teenage Mutant Ninja Turtles punching bag that stood as tall as me. One night, I was upstairs in my bedroom and decided I was going to draw the punching bag on a piece of paper. I sat on my bed that evening and spent several hours, before and after dinner, drawing the punching bag's characters in detail. I was so excited and impressed with my creation that I rushed downstairs to show my dad. I remember handing it to him and his energy and facial expressions immediately turned to anger.

"Did you do this?"

"Yes, Dad."

He shook his head in disgust. He did not believe me. "If you ever trace and lie to me again …"

He then took my drawing and ripped it into pieces. It destroyed me. I don't know what hurt me more – the fact that he had just ripped up my drawing that I had spent so much time creating or the fact that he didn't believe I could do it. I mean, the paper was eleven inches by eight and a half inches and the punching bag was at least five feet tall. You couldn't even trace it if you tried. Looking back, he had probably been drinking, as he often did. He was unhappy and dealing with his own demons. Unfortunately, the damage was done, I never wanted to lift a pencil again. I buried that passion of mine so deep that I forgot about it for most of my adult life. At that point, I never wanted to create again. This would all change though.

In my mid-thirties, I had become an avid art collector, developing friendships with some of Los Angeles's finest artists of our generation. I was also actively involved with organizations like MOCA and attended a lot of events. I love being involved in this world. I had always been a very imaginative and creative businessman, which I feel has given me the vision to lead successful companies. Being a part of events like these and being surrounded by professional artists, brought something out in me that I hadn't felt in a really long time, back to the days of the young boy making Ninja Turtles drawings. It made me want to create again.

I remember being home, late in the evening. I was not tired, and I didn't feel like reading a book or doing any work. The fireplace was going in my bedroom. I had just had my custom bedroom set, which I had designed, delivered. I was sitting in one of my dark gray oversized chairs; I had my feet up on the matching ottoman. Something inside of me told me to grab a notebook and a pencil. I don't know why, but Jerry from *Tom and Jerry* came into my mind. I picked up my iPhone and I googled the famed cartoon. I immediately began to sketch out the little mouse. It was almost perfect. I realized that even though I hadn't drawn in so long, I still had this gift (if that's what you want to call it). Over the next several days, I started sketching and drawing again; I felt that I was starting to be really creative.

I then had this crazy idea a few weeks later. I told a well-known artist friend of mine that he should produce a painting using a fine wine in my cellar. "Why don't you use the wine from an expensive bottle and mix it with the paint? Since it is painted on a large-scale contemporary canvas, the wine will literally last forever." I suggested he take a 1985 Sassicaia, a Cabernet Sauvignon from

Tuscany, reputed to be the best vintage in Italian history and costs more than $4,000 a bottle. (A little further in this book, I'm going to tell you more about how my love affair with fine wine began, and how I went on to build the luxury wine brand called King of Clubs.)

"I can't do that. That's your idea, plus you are the wine connoisseur, you should do it," he encouraged.

It was like a sudden lighting strike; it was exactly what I was hoping he would say without even knowing it. I think my subconscious was manifesting something that I needed. I went to the art store in West Hollywood and bought a large roll of raw canvas and Golden Heavy Body acrylic paints, mainly royal blues, metallic blues, white, and gold. I rolled this five-and-a-half foot by twelve-foot canvas out in my kitchen and started to apply a few coats of gesso.

I was excited with anticipation for what I might create. I was not dwelling on the thought that some might feel that this was sacrilegious, though the notion clearly came to mind.

Once the canvas was ready and the gesso had dried, I put on some Frank Sinatra. I poured myself a tiny glass of the '85 and let it settle on my tongue. Ah, I could sense the vanilla, ripe cherries, blackberries, and cinnamon. This beautiful scene was unfolding in my quiet kitchen, with nothing but the soundtrack of my life playing in this moment. I can remember it like it was yesterday, it was late in the evening after the kids were asleep. Was I really going to use this expensive bottle of wine – sought-after by connoisseurs - and simply mix it in the paint and even toss some of it on this canvas? Undeterred, I started to mix the wine into all of the Golden Heavy paints that I had carefully already poured out into buckets.

With Ole Blue Eyes crooning "Fly Me to the Moon," I stood for several minutes just contemplating the blank canvas. What was I going to do? Then I started to apply some dribbles of blue. At first, I wasn't sure how it might look. But then, I grew bolder, working long circular strokes, across the canvas. I just let go. I felt an amazing sense of release as I watched every spatter hit the white canvas. I used spoons, brushes, knives, and kitchen utensils. It was this overwhelming balance of fear and excitement. It almost felt like an out-of-body experience. The music made me sway and this helped the swirls of paint drop like clef-marks of an ultra-smooth jazz dream. Then I turned up the music even louder, really in the moment. All of the childhood self-doubts and negativity washed away, as I remained focused on this swirling movement and color. It was hypnotizing. It was my personal homage to Sassicaia and Pollock, and it was a rite of passage for me.

When Pollock[1] spoke of his "action art," he explained that he never touched the canvas as it lay on the floor. "I hardly ever stretch my canvas before painting. I prefer to tack the unstretched canvas to the hard wall or the floor; I need the resistance of a hard surface. On the floor I am more at ease." I stood in my kitchen, with my paintbrush, kitchen utensils, and wine as a vessel, slowly removing away the years of not being creative, of not taking action about something I used to love so much as a kid.

Then, with my whole canvas covered, I squirted the last remaining drops of '85, staining various spots across the canvas. Apart from my earlier mouthful, which still lingered, the canvas soaked up a whole bottle of the '85. The artistic point for me was that this vintage was being locked into the painting for as long as the artwork would exist. I kept the bottle, complete with blue spots of my fingertips from the paint, and placed it in a Perspex case that will remain with the framed painting as a sort of official seal of authenticity. The whole experience allowed me to exorcise my childhood fears and made me think that nothing in life should hold you back. If you want to do something, get up and do it. After all, failure is not even trying in the first place. I completed the canvas and left it to settle for a few days before examining it. Did I like it? Yes. Did I love it? I was not sure. I sensed there was something not quite right. The perfectionist and creator in me wanted this to be more than just art, after all, it had the greatness of this wine in its veins. I added some extra streaks of gold, giving it a regal feel. More importantly, I realized that I was capable of being the creator that I always wanted to be. To this day, this painting is framed and hanging in my living room as a constant reminder for me to be bold, to follow my dreams, and never ever stop creating!

I love my sons so much. Zachary is eight, and Cruz is seven. They mean everything to me. I was driving them to their school in Beverly Hills a few years back, and they were in the backseat of my white Mulsanne Speed. As we cruised down through the morning traffic, Cruz stuck a little Lego man figure inside the air conditioning vent. This is never a good thing to do in an expensive vehicle like this. The dealership charges an arm-and-a-leg to fix anything. It wouldn't come out and Cruz started to get upset. When we came up to the traffic light, I reached behind and stuck my fingers into the vent, and I tried to take out the Lego piece.

"Daddy, daddy, I have small fingers. I can get it out," said my oldest son Zachary. Most parents will appreciate what I was wanting to say next, "No son, you can't do that. Daddy will get it later."

I stopped myself before I spoke though. I had an instant flashback to my own childhood. I was told not to do certain things; I remember the effect it had on me. Instead, I smiled and I looked back over my shoulder at Zachary.

"Okay, son, go for it!"

I sat up straight in my seat to see him in the mirror working effortlessly to slip his little fingers into the space. I could make out his wrist wiggling as his fingers disappeared for a moment. He pulled the Lego piece out very quickly. He held it up and his face was beaming with a broad smile.

"Look, Daddy. Look. I got it out!"

"Zachary, look at my boy, Daddy is so proud of you."

His brother, Cruz, also broke into a laughing smile as he was handed back the Lego figure. I knew at that moment that by encouraging these young boys, as opposed to the way I had been treated as a child, that they would feel loved and empowered to do better things. To be successful in life, we need to be aware that we may have skeletons in our proverbial closet that may cause us to do or say things that don't actually support the very people we love the most.

Never be ashamed of where you started or what you had to go through in life to make something of yourself. The "past" is part of your story, but like I said in the beginning of this chapter, it doesn't define who you are today or even tomorrow.

Getting the Job Done

Let me share another story of one of my first jobs. It all started in a warehouse in Massachusetts. Even by warehouse standards, the C&S Wholesale Grocers off of Highway 91 is massive. A gray shed of over a million square feet surrounded by barbed-wire fencing is in clear view as you land at Bradley International Airport. In 1996, C&S was one of the major warehouses for Wal-Mart, Pathmark, A&Ps, Safeway, and the major supermarkets. This was an enormous plant with hundreds of trucks constantly coming and going, passing through the guardhouse, and heading out the back into King Spring Road. The west side of the building had over fifty loading bays for trucks. This was a supplier for grocery stores, full of dairy, meat, and frozen foods. I spent nearly a year riding around on the platform of a motorized pallet-jack. Each driver buzzed between the maze of shelving, picking pallets for different orders for individual stores. Drivers made their money on how they picked the pallets and how quickly they could fulfill them. There were a lot of guys trying to make their orders and make a buck.

It was a jungle in there. This was like Russell Crow in "Gladiator." This was one of the life experiences that really hardened people. You had to hustle. The autumn weather was changing into winter as I began my two-week training on how to steer and lift pallets, earning twelve dollars an hour. But once training was over, I was placed on a team and my wage depended on the average amount shipped out by the team. As days got colder and darker, the temperatures plummeted far below freezing, and in the massive warehouse the limited heat escaped through the gigantic bay doors. My bare hands jarred with the cold when I touched metal or wood.

Countless times my fingers would crack enough to cause pain but not enough to keep bleeding.

There was a point that most people would just break, but this was going to toughen me up. I had to bring in money. I told myself that there were going to be future opportunities, I wanted to earn and save, so I was prepared to grab it. Inside, I raced around the aisles on the edge of twin-forked pallet-jacks, weaving, and dodging other guys. I would get long sheets of stickers and a product number. I had to run around empty pallets, put the sticker on the product, and stack the product on these pallet jacks. As you were building the pallets, you had to cover them in shrink wrap. I was paid ten cents a sticker. I thought about how much work I might have to do to make a few thousand dollars. I don't remember how many pallets a day I would get to, however, if you looked outside of the C&S warehouse, there were probably forty to seventy-five tractor trailer trucks every day that had to be packed. You were racing against the clock, wrapping the pallet and trying to get it back to the docking bay in time. It was all based on speed, time, and how you picked.

Back then, it was one of the few places where you could work legitimately and make $50,000 - $60,000 a year without a degree or even a high school diploma. You have these rough personality types and aggressive people all racing to make a living. While other guys my age were in college and lecture halls studying history, business, engineering, or the law, I was in this high-tension atmosphere. I stuck it out for close to a year. I worked twelve to eighteen-hour shifts, four days a week. The day shift started at 5:00 a.m. and was a chaotic and frantic rush. The night shift was much quieter as the large shelves were replenished once again, before the morning onslaught.

This was no joke; it was hard labor. There was a rush to get the best pallet-jacks. You still had to work fast even if you ended up with a slow one, jumping off while they were still running. My sense of humor helped me survive, showing I was strong-minded. The guys would build home-made boom boxes, so naturally I ended up building my own boom-box with speakers connected to the battery. I would play the latest hip-hop tracks of A Tribe Called Quest, De La Soul and Busta Rhymes, which allowed me to get into a groove and excel. Though there were freezing temperatures, I was in shorts and a tank top sweating from the long shifts. I mean we would pick thousands of items. There was a high staff turn-around, plenty of guys were unable to cut it. I did really well and took home some healthy pay checks.

My ethos was: *You have to get it done. There are no excuses, just get the job done.* I got to know a lot of solid guys with street-life camaraderie and practical joking. It was fun and games, but we also had to making sure no one got themselves killed or injured, which was no small feat, a lot of guys got seriously injured. The pallet jacks were fast and the guys would work at intense speeds, crisscrossing and moving busily to make a paycheck. Sometimes this competitive tension spilled over and there would be a scuffle and even a few punches thrown. However, no one wanted to be thrown out of an opportunity to make good money, so it was always brief. It taught me about sticking it out – and never quitting. I really believe that it was these early experiences that made me fearless. Something like eighty percent of the people who started quit within the first week. I felt that if I could endure working in this kind of place, while making some money – then I felt I could do anything. I wasn't going to let my current situation and past mistakes define where I was going and what I would do with my life!

IV. EMBRACE CHANGE

Everybody craves change. No matter how big or small, we all want to change. It can be for a better career, newer car, bigger home, change in our health, and even our fitness goals. Yet somehow, we are all afraid of it. We reject it, and find that the steps to create change can be difficult and even seem impossible at times. However, change is an important part of your growth and is necessary to excel and move forward in life. I know first-hand how uncomfortable it can be, but for you to truly become the person you are meant to be, you need to allow change in your life. Change means progress and is essential to reach your goals and dreams.

Change has been a constantly moving landscape for me. It's been like driving on the highway across America and watching the scenery shift and evolve every mile of the journey. My life has been a series of major transitions that have all accelerated me to where I am today. I picked up everything and moving from Connecticut to Atlanta, and then had an even bigger transition when I moved away from friends and family to California. It was not only a long way from home and a different time zone, but I didn't really know anyone here. Little did I know that when I moved to Los Angeles, in just one month, an impactful incident would happen to me.

It was just a little more than forty-five days after moving to California, that my grandmother Jean had a bad fall and needed to have hip surgery. She was admitted to the hospital and underwent a successful operation, unfortunately, her body suffered trauma that could not be overcome. I had this feeling that I had to be there. So I decided to come home to see her and be with my family for Thanksgiving. My mother picked me up at the airport, and we headed straight to the hospital.

I walked into the room to see her lying in bed. She looked up with a big smile. My grandmother or "Nanny" as we would call her, didn't smile often. She gave us tough love, and a smile from her was worth everything, especially at this time.

She raised her two children, but then also her three grandchildren, who were my cousins. She became their legal guardian. When my father left and things became difficult, we moved in with her. My mother was working a full-time job, and after school Nanny would watch us until she got home. This tough woman raised two generations. She cooked, cleaned, and held down the house. There were seven of us living under that roof at one point. As strong as she was, and with all that she had been through, today she looked weak and tired. I sat down next to her after a long hug. She wanted some milk, and the nurses were not responding. I remember holding back the tears and yelling out, "Can someone please get her some milk!" It was my turn to be strong for her.

We started to chat and she kept saying how tired she was. I could sense this might be the last time I would ever see her. It was hard for me. She did so much for so many people. She was the definition of a strong woman who led her family, but old age and what she recently had gone through had taken its toll.

After several hours, I left the hospital to head back to my mother's. I had dinner with my family that evening and left early the next morning to go back to LA.

On December 1, 2009, I was about to go for my morning run

when the phone rang. I saw that it was my mother and something didn't feel right.

I picked up, "Hey Mom."

She didn't even speak for thirty seconds; I could hear her crying. Let me preface this by saying that my mother is also a really strong woman like Nanny.

"Christopher, Nanny is gone, she went to heaven today." I lost it, I felt like I couldn't breathe. I shouldn't have left. I questioned myself. *Why wasn't I there?* I couldn't hold back the tears. This hit me hard.

In my grief, I remembered everything that she used to tell me. She used to tell me to clean up my act and make everyone proud. She would tell me that I was special and had so much potential. I remember being back home to visit her years prior. I was proud of the successes that I had in Atlanta. I would visit with her, leaving money hidden in her books and putting extra in her wallet. She would often say to me, you need to settle down, find a good woman, and have children. There were so many memories, so many stories, and now it was over. Her life had changed me, and now her death had even more of an impact on me. These momentous events would change me forever. As they say, I now finally realized, "Tomorrow is never promised," and it was time to put my life in overdrive.

Her memory and gentle nudging (sometimes not so gentle!) led me to settle down and get married. Unfortunately, my marriage didn't work. As always, my mindset is to be positive, and even though the divorce was difficult, I see the silver lining. In this case, it was that we are the parents of two healthy and amazing sons. I've made it a point, now that I am a single father, to do the best possible job I can do co-parenting with their mom and continuing to provide for them the life I always imagined they would have. Meanwhile, I remain an incurable romantic, and I know that the perfect partner is out there for me somewhere.

I believe in reinvention and there has never been a moment in my life where I thought I had it all. I've always remained open-minded and willing to learn new things or steer off in a new direction. I think being prepared to constantly evolve and change has allowed me to bounce back quickly from failures and devastating blows. It has given me a sense of resilience. I truly encourage you, as a reader, to build your own inner strength and embrace change. You might not always have the disposition and energy to embrace change. However, I implore you, change is something that you must get comfortable with.

This goes for my kids too. I want them to experience change even at their age. I'm encouraging them to be better human beings. I teach them to be more patient, respectful, and to commit to learn things they don't know or even like. Don't all parents want that? You are either evolving and changing every day or you are lost and stuck. Believe me, change is generally a good thing.

I read a book called *Change or Die*[1]. It spoke about how you must constantly evolve your craft or you get left behind. Even today, as you read this, my craft is changing, and I'm embracing it. I don't believe that we are supposed to be just one thing. I have done so many things, and there is still so much to do. There's always going to be that pivotal moment in your life requiring change. Too often we're afraid to admit it. Embracing and surrendering to the fear of the unknown is the very start of change.

It's Not How Good You Are, It's How Good You Want to Be[2] by Paul Arden is another book that helped me to embrace change. It was given to me as a present by my friend Jim, an early mentor in Atlanta. Ironically, it was also given to me again by Rob Drydek a few Christmases ago. Jim, this charismatic guy was like a father figure to me at that time in my life. He and his beautiful wife were impeccably dressed every day. I admired them. I loved their home and its Parisian décor which was always a delight to be in. They had a phenomenal bond and chemistry. I really respected Jim, so when he gifted me this book, I took it seriously. Its single nugget of advice: *Don't take no for an answer*.

When I was a boy, I picked up something pretty fundamental from watching one of my favorite movies, Martin Scorsese's *Good-fellas*. "Be a man of your word." Developing my own sense of loyalty and respect for others has been fundamental to my success and made me change my outlook on life.

Many of these authors talk about change from a wider perspective, but not one person or company is immune to it. Some of the world's largest corporate firms have failed spectacularly because they ignored that the entire world was changing. Silicon Valley refers to it as "disruption," which is simply another fancy word for change. It's the same for human beings. Even during this time, as I am finally releasing this book, the world is in the midst of some of the greatest changes.

How do we embrace change? It seems so obvious: We must tell the truth about the way we all live, and do something positive about it. Nothing less.

Change, Italian Style

I was about to transition into a period of awakening and realization that would physically change me forever. In 2013, I was in Italy for the first time, on a week-long sojourn through Roma to Capri. I checked off a few things on my bucket list, one of which, was driving a Ferrari along the twisting and turning scenic Amalfi Coast and seeing the Vatican and the great Colosseum. I remember falling in love with the energy, the architecture, the food, and more importantly, the people. I was sightseeing and taking this beautiful city in. I recall discovering the Largo di Torre Argentina. This is the place where Emperor Caesar was betrayed by his closest friend, Brutus, and was stabbed twenty-two times outside of the Theater of Pompey and killed.

There was so much history and inspiration in this city. As I walked around shopping and saw more legendary tourist places, I ate fresh mozzarella, juicy, ripened organic tomatoes, locally-made pasta, and fresh fish every day. At its most authentic, Italian food is simple, freshly made, and delicious. I remember getting the recommendation from the hotel to try Pierluigi. Little did I know that another change was about to take place in my life.

I arrived at the restaurant with no reservation and asked to see the wine cellar. I was with my ex-girlfriend at the time. We wanted a special, romantic lunch with some wine. I asked if we could sit in the cellar after holding two expensive bottles in my hand, the 1989 Sassicaia and 1989 Gaja Barbaresco. The restaurant's manager, Alessandro Tibaldo, came down to open the wine and introduce himself. We had ordered so much food: langoustines, pasta, and oysters. The food was like nothing I ever had, it was so fresh and full of flavor.

Alessandro remembers that day very well:

A famous hotel in Rome called us to reserve a table. A VIP table, they said. Here at Pierluigi, it is not unusual to get this kind of request. But no one knew, or could have imagined by then, that this particular guest would become a great friend! It was a Thursday lunch; I remember it well. You don't often get clients reserving the entire Wine Room, with over 2,400 labels. Let alone on a Thursday lunch. But he does! Needless to say, we were all impatient to see who was coming, and what was this all about! He arrives at 1:15 p.m. punctual as a star. When he gets out of his luxury Mercedes, wearing a Borsalino hat and a dazzling smile, he really looks like a star. Maybe from one of Fellini's movies. Then she comes, his girlfriend at the time. She's astonishing, so lovely! They are so beautiful; you're left with nothing but wondering ... Is this La Dolce Vita?

He wastes no time and asks for the wine list. He orders three bottles. "You can open them all," he says. "But I'm only going to drink one now and please decant the other two. I want to drink them tonight," he says. He asks, "Would you mind reserving your best outdoor table for us tonight? And could you make sure there is a bouquet of red roses on it?" I was speechless and amazed. He was so egocentric, so overconfident. Or perhaps he was truly in love with this girl? Who's this guy? "Mr. King," he says. He sticks his hand out, he shakes mine. "I'm Mr. King." When they came back, that night, they found the best table we had to offer, in one of the most iconic piazzas in Rome, the Piazza dei Ricci. The woman was even more stunning in an elegant dress. You would expect some paparazzi to come out of nowhere, only to flash them quickly before they run away in their fancy car. The wine is ready but before taking a sip, Mr. King wants to make sure we all get a glass. It is his special night, and that is his way to thank us for making it so perfect. Are we already friends by then? Does it take only half of a day to connect so deeply with someone? Perhaps it takes a great bottle of wine or two or three or many. Perhaps it only takes that great passion for wine that we have in common.

The passion we share has brought us together in Rome for many years now, and we continue to meet at Pierluigi every time Mr. King is in town. When we get together, we are always ready to pop another great bottle (or two or three). It's always great to see our dear friend Mr. King!

This wonderful restaurant was founded in 1938 by Umberto Pierluigi. Originally an osteria, it is located in Piazza de' Ricci in the center of Rome. In its privileged position over the years, it has frequently updated its menus and has created this elegant venue on demand by locals, and clients of international stature. In 1980, young Roberto Lisi, took over the property and kept the name. He embarked on an evolutionary path that transformed the small family-run trattoria into an upscale restaurant. A decade later, Roberto became a pioneer among the Roman culinary scene. This delicious and elegant hot spot is one for all who love the very best that Roma has to offer.

After this spectacular meal, I took Alessandro aside and told him, "I love this food, it's the best thing I've ever had!"

Since this day, the owner Lorenzo, Alessandro, and I have become close friends, like brothers. I have been back to the restaurant several times and have also visited his newly opened hotel, Hotel di Ricci. After long workdays in Milan, I often take the two-hour train ride just to have dinner with them. We eat, drink wine, and catch up. Recently I was there discussing life and businesses as usual with Lorenzo. I was excited to see the chef, Alessandro, and the whole team. I had just met fellow LA neighbors at the restaurant, Freddy and Jaqueline, who share the same passion as I do for Italy. We were all laughing and enjoying the evening. The occasion marked the very first time I tried Tua Rita Redigaffi. Now, keep in mind that I can be stubborn. I love what I love, and it's hard to change my mind. I wanted the Masseto and wasn't budging. However, Alessandro insisted, "Mr. King, please brother, you must be open to change and try something new." I laughed and said, "Of course brother." Change at that time led me to learn about a new wine in Italy. With its cult following, the Redigaffi is considered one of the country's best Merlots and is to die for; it quickly became one of my favorites.

I have enough stories, laughs, and memories that could fill an entire new book. Lorenzo, Cristina, and their two dogs are like an extended family to me. To top it all off, I am so excited that Lorenzo recently announced that he is opening a restaurant in Los Angeles.

On these trips to Italy, though I enjoyed the food immensely, I actually lost weight. I even remember on that very first trip to Italy that I didn't get sick. I didn't need my acid reflex pills that I often took after dining in America. It was utterly amazing. Why? The food was fresh. There are no food preservatives; GMO is basically illegal in Italy. You can buy a gallon of milk and it spoils in a few days, not like in America where it somehow can last a month. It was this drastic change in food philosophy that caused a major effect on my health and my body.

I had been having health difficulties for years. I was in a bad car accident which left me with significant back issues. I couldn't walk for almost three months due to this injury. This was the time when Zachary was just born. I used to walk and rock him to sleep but couldn't anymore because of this injury and excruciating pain. I was told that I needed to have disc replacement surgery in order for me to be able to run or be active again. I decided against this invasive course of action, and instead I chose to undergo rehabilitation and physical therapy, to strengthen my core and work on rebuilding my back.

I used to love running long-distance, it was something that I would often do to clear my mind early in the mornings. But I could no longer make these runs. My life had changed and I ended up putting on weight.

This was a turning point in my life, and I knew I had to make changes. There is no question that health is wealth. One of the most important changes that we can ever make is to take care of our bodies just as much as our mind. Even though many years have passed since the accident, I was still making excuses. I needed to make conscious and uncomfortable changes if I was going to drop the weight and regain my health. Like anything in life, when I want to make a major change, I dive all-in with research. I also started looking into why the food in Italy was so different and why I didn't react the same way I did with the food here in America. Not only did I want to change the foods I was eating, but I also had to change my workout routine. I trained with weights differently, managed my diet, and ultimately, results came quickly. People even have asked me if I had work done, such as Botox and so forth. I also believe that it led to improve my mood. I was happier, with less stress, which affected me physically as well. I was eventually able to run again and even signed up and completed a half marathon recently. It goes to show that when you commit to make a change and follow through, anything is possible.

V. READ THE FINE PRINT

In 1995, my life-long friend Ray and I were determined to make it on our own. We had this undeniable bond: our love of basketball, the hustle to make something out of our lives, and our family situations brought us together. Our moms were single mothers, who had done what they could by themselves. Without father figures to guide us, Ray and I did our best. We were independent kids trying to find our way. We knew we didn't want to be broke and poor, and it was frustrating to not be able to afford the newest clothing and sneakers. Let's be frank, we were hustlers. We did whatever it took to figure out a money-making business, and most of our ideas failed. However, let me assure you that we never gave up. As teenagers, Ray and I would cut grass in the summer or shovel snow from old folks' driveways in the winter just to keep money coming in between our big business ideas. We would take any opportunity that came along to make a few dollars. I've always believed in the value of hard work. We had bills to pay and a lifestyle to fund.

I needed wheels! So, I poured my savings into my first car: a cream Ford Thunderbird that was fairly rusty on the passenger side door and needed repair. I did it myself because I didn't have the money for a professional job. I wasn't sure what to do, but I knew it needed to be done. I went to the local Pep Boys, bought the sandpaper and the bondo filler. (This was before YouTube showed you how to do it!) After reading the instructions on the can, I dove in headfirst. It was with the same determination I still show today when faced with a challenge or something unknown. I always figure it out and find a way. I chipped away the rust with a small hammer, hand-sanded the area, applied the filler, and waited for it to set. I sanded again and smoothed the final layers. Then I painted the Ford with a primer gray. After saving a bit more money, I got the car professionally sprayed brilliant white and added some original wheels. It was official, I was in business with my very first ride! Now that I was mobile, Ray and I decided to set up our own business. We didn't know what type of business, until a big red pick-up truck with a slick logo zoomed past, filled with high-powered lawnmowers, weed whackers, and bags of bush and tree cuttings. That was it.

"Let's get a landscaping business going. We've cut grass before. How hard can it be?" I said. That was our first business, and while Ray had doubts on how we would start the business, he saw the opportunity. More importantly, we saw the money we could make.

We added a third partner, who was a close friend and we managed to secure a $5,000 loan through a local bank. We bought a used GMC pick-up with a trailer, a lawnmower, and a few extra pieces of equipment, like weed whackers and hedge trimers. We started by cutting lawns, trimming bushes and picking up leaves for residential homes, and eventually, we were able to expand to businesses in three different towns and cities in Connecticut. This was my earliest opportunity to try out my marketing skills and experiment with creative branding. I took the time to design and create the logo, letterhead, flyers, and marketing material. I wanted it to look official.

This was the east coast in the middle of summer. It was humid and over ninety degrees. We were out there up to fifteen hours a day, cutting grass, trimming bushes, snipping, cutting, and hauling.

We were perfectionists in every aspect of the job, even measuring each bush to ensure that it was straight. We wanted to do a good job, so we would get rehired and get referrals. Our shoulders, arms, and backs would hurt until we had a few drinks at a local Chinese restaurant which would ease our pain. We would kick back a few Blue Hawaiians with rum, Blue Curacao, pineapple juice, coconut, and ice. We would share a Scorpion Bowl: a concoction of various gins, dark rum and light rum, vodka, grenadine, and orange juice in a large dish with a flame of 151 proof rum as the fiery showpiece. I think you get the picture! Finally, we would order a generous serving of General Tso's Chicken to help us rebuild our strength. Somehow, we would get up the next day to do it all over again.

Our summer was going really well and in no time our landscaping business had the opportunity to land its first – and only – major commercial account with a fitness center called Bally Total Fitness in East Hartford. Other young guys were running around doing what we were doing – I wanted us to be bigger and better than them. I was pushing to get us to the next level quicker than anyone else. That fire inside of me was already driving me. I wanted to grow, add trucks, generate more revenue, get more employees. We wanted to live a good life and care for our moms and family. Nothing was going to stop us. We were going to land this account.

We pulled up outside Bally and parked our pick-up, which leaked oil in summer and anti-freeze in the winter. Around the fringe of the parking lot was a landscaped area of grass and trees merging next to a busy gas station next door. I had heard that they were considering re-doing the landscape design here, as well as with their facilities in West Hartford and New Britain. This was such a great opportunity, and we were going for it. We were ushered into the manager's office, while customers were working out with weights and machines. In full salesman mode, I politely thanked the manager for this potential opportunity. Introductions were made, and then we pitched them about what we could do for Bally Total

Fitness. It went great, and we subsequently won the account to do not one, but two Bally Fitness centers!

The three of us could not believe we had landed a deal; we joked around and slapped each other's back as we headed to the parking lot to our beat-up truck. We were excited to get right to work. I felt like we had the business side in order. I was constantly on the go and always on the phone trying to close more deals and negotiate all of the materials we were going to need for this big job. I had bought a Motorola flip phone from a Jamaican street seller in Hartford, which went for $200 back then. I had free usage for several months until it was shut down – after that, I had to get a proper pay-as-you-go cell for the business.

After I closed the Bally deal, we went to the timber supplier to get the wood, the mulch, and all the other materials. One small problem was that we didn't have any real capital. We were seventeen-year-old kids and had already used up our loan money to buy our equipment. Being the creative minds that we were, we managed to get a thirty-day term with the suppliers. To this day, I have no idea how I managed to sell that one to the store manager! We figured that the first check from Bally's would be good enough to repay all the suppliers and leave us a hefty profit. We would look like heroes, and it would all go smoothly. However, those thirty days came around very quickly and the suppliers wanted their money, yet our payment from the health club hadn't arrived. I started to get anxious and went down to the location to speak with the manager.

I remember the manager bringing out the contract and turned to the terms section and pointed out the very obvious 120-day term for all vendors right there in writing. My heart sank. We had made our first fatal mistake. The contract had clearly said 120 days, so we had done all the work and couldn't get paid until then. Forget the weeks of hard labor in the blistering sun, we were screwed! We hadn't looked properly at our agreement, and we realized the health club did not have to pay us for another three months, yet we were now in substantial debt to our suppliers. We eventually got paid and settled our accounts. However, the business didn't last, and we couldn't continue to operate. This was my first setback and a valuable lesson. *Read the small print! Make sure you know exactly what you are getting yourself into. Prepare for success, not failure.*

I am often described as a person who picks up on the finest details. However, every now and then you can find yourself in a situation of not paying attention and overlooking something. Instead of letting it ruin your plans, look at it as an opportunity to find a solution, which can lead to a change for the better. Fast forward to one of my first trips to Paris, I am an unabashed duck lover. No one does it better than Michelin-starred chef, Alain Ducasse. For many food lovers, Alain is the godfather of French gastronomy and alongside the late, great Joel Robuchon, is the only chef to garner more than twenty Michelin stars for his finely prepared and presented food. His famed restaurant is in the Hotel Plaza Athénée on avenue Montaigne in Paris. It was recommended to me after I arrived. I took with me a bottle of Petrus 2001, an Appellation Pomerol Contrôlée. (For the uninitiated, it is a fabulous and rather expensive bottle of wine.) I recently had bought a case of the 2001 vintage at auction, and I decided to take two bottles to Paris with me. Ducasse's signature dish is the duck, and this is what I was craving and frankly, expecting. However, when I arrived at the hotel, I had no idea I was walking into a vegetarian restaurant. The dining room was one of the finest I've ever been to with its silver and white theme design by Patrick Jouin and Sanjit Manku. Even the cutlery, created exclusively for this restaurant by Roger Tallon in the 1970s, was a pleasure to handle. However, it seemed this great chef had become a little bored with meat and had decided to experiment with a vegetarian menu. His goal was to do the impossible and get another Michelin star as a vegetarian restaurant. I hadn't been following the French media and was unaware of his recent shift in focus.

I hadn't taken the time to check the basics! (There is a lesson to learn here.) I had however, taken two or three fine Cuban cigars with me. I had bought them around the corner from the George V

Hotel in a Parisian tabac called A La Civette on rue St. Honoré. Now, I was sitting comfortably in Ducasse's restaurant. I had a few Maduro Number 5's, one of my favorite smokes, and my bottle of Petrus. What could be better? It's at that moment that I realized that the menu was all vegetarian. Alain, in his monogrammed chef's whites, his striking head of gray hair, with his spectacles in hand, came out of the kitchen to say hello.

"Alain, I have a tiny problem," I ventured, rather nervously.

"What is it, monsieur, and how can we fix it?"

"Well, one of my great culinary friends in California recommended that I come here to eat. I've made a special trip here, but I am looking at your menu, and it's all vegetarian!"

"Mais oui, that's correct."

"But I've been dying for you to make that famous duck … and you decided to change it up on me." He laughed and looked down at the unopened bottle of Petrus. He pointed.

"Let's open this up and I'll have a glass with you. And I'll take one of those cigars, and I'll make you duck."

"It's a deal," I responded.

He headed back to his kitchen and made a special duck dish for me. It was sensational in a beautiful orange sauce. It melted in my mouth. I will never forget it. It was the best duck I have ever had in my life. Paired with the beautiful Petrus, it was frankly the meal of a lifetime. To top it off, after dinner, I was offered the chance to go and inspect the kitchen and watch Alain and his team at work. We got the opportunity to share some stories and laughs together. It was a chance to learn some of the secrets from this great chef and how he created such perfection on a plate. Of course, you don't need a trip to Paris, or a meal at Alain Ducasse to get the point I am trying to make. Wherever you are, the lesson here is the same. Turning a miss into an opportunity will create a lifetime moment that you won't forget. Refocusing after a setback, whether it is missing some important details, or failing to read the small print, will always allow you to thrive regardless of the circumstances.

VI. DRESS FOR SUCCESS

One of the first and most valuable lessons that I've learned as a successful entrepreneur was that you have to dress for success. The way you dress is a reflection of who you are. It's a form of respect and in my travels has been a key to starting conversations and being taken serious in business. As you know by now, I didn't grow up with any male role models. Like a lot of young men without proper guidance, I had to figure it out on my own. I started to developed my own style from magazines and book images and after guys I saw in the movies like *Goodfellas*, *The Godfather* trilogy, and all the cool guys from the old Rat Pack days, guys like Frank Sinatra, Clark Gable, and Humphrey Bogart.

I was living in Hartford, Connecticut, at the Bushnell Tower on the seventeenth floor. As kids we would drive by looking and dreaming about what it would be like to live there, and now I was actually living in this incredible condo. This was when I first started to introduce suits into my wardrobe. It was also the first time that I was able to understand how it made me feel while wearing one. It was a normal weekday, I had to make a very important call from my house – this was a make-it-or-break-it kind of call. I decided that even if it was from my home office, I would get up early, shower, and got fully dressed in my suit with shoes, cufflinks, and pochette; I even wore cologne to take the call. It made me take the call more seriously, I also sounded more professional, and it helped boost my self-esteem.

This is about building your self-confidence and preparing for success at any level from any situation. Someone speaking to me on a conference call from thousands of miles away is unlikely to know that I am wearing a particular cologne or that my shoes are polished for the call, but these details matter to me. It's about respect and taking the time to care. I have had many more of these calls and no matter what, I am always properly prepared. What's surprising is that every time I had those calls, I would close ninety-nine percent of the deals. Try it for yourself and watch how very different that conversation goes for you. This attitude and mindset allow me to make the best of every situation. It has become part of my daily routine which continues to evolve over time.

Just remember, we all have to start somewhere. I was introduced to a young kid whose family had a tailor business in a local suit shop called K&G. In East Hartford, this was the place to buy suits for very little money. We would buy the suit and he would hook us up by tailoring it for us. I had to work my way from a $99 suit to a $200 Jones New York suit up to Armani, until I was able to afford the suits I have and wear today. I would take these affordable suits down to my tailor and work on making sure it fit properly. Suiting is all about fit. Find yourself a great tailor, and watch him change the way you look. It will make you enjoy wearing it and feel comfortable.

As I've established, I didn't come from money. So, for me it was about looking as sharp as I could afford. I have learned so much since those days going through trial and error. I've learned about fabric, sizes, style, horn buttons versus plastic ones, various lapel and collar styles, etc. I can tell you this, if you make the investment in well-made clothing and even shoes or bags, they will last a life-time. I know this because I still have quality items that I still wear and use that are over twelve years old. It's also about taking care of these quality pieces and learning how to properly launder and store them.

The same can be said about the way women dress. I have many friends, like Max Girombelli in New York City who also makes bespoke tailoring for ladies. His company Duca Satoria makes a custom suit for both – the rules for quality and fit apply to both men and women. Dressing for success is for everyone.

I was around twenty-three when I knew I wanted to wear a suit every day. My personal taste was fixed on those double-breasted, pin-striped, peak lapel suits just like the guys in those old gangster movies. I felt like they were the personification of style, class and power. The old saying by Thomas Fuller is still a quote in my office, "Good clothes open all doors." I still think this is true, yet too many people don't seem to appreciate this.

From those early years, making intentional choices about what I wore and how I wore it made a remarkable difference. I realized that if I was wearing a sharp suit and crisp shirt, it was easier to make a good first impression. Don't get me wrong, there are times and places for casual dressing. A nice pair of jeans, sneakers and shirt can be stylish and leave an impression. However, I learned this: You can never dress up in a room, but you can always dress down. Even now, I always want to be the sharpest dressed man in any room. It's not to show off or think that I am better than anyone else; it's for myself; it's just how I am wired.

As my business was growing rapidly in Atlanta, this is when I really started to pay attention. I was at a Lamborghini event that was thrown by my good friend Ryan Hattaway. I was there looking sharp in jeans, some custom Gucci loafers, a crisp white shirt, and a gray jacket I had tailored. It was a chilly night in Atlanta that evening, so I accessorized with a black and grey Gucci scarf. I was there for a few minutes enjoying a cocktail when a man approached me and said, "Sir excuse me. You look amazing, but you are missing just one thing." He reached into his front pocket and removed a pocket square, or as I like to call it, a pochette. As he put it in my pocket, he said, "Now you look complete." Not only did he gift me his pochette, but as you can imagine, he quickly became my tailor and then a great friend. Mark Fonseca of Fonseca Clothiers was my first custom tailor and was making power suits for Atlanta's who's who. It was a matter of weeks before we ended up sitting down and going through the process of picking and making my very first bespoke suit. I remember it like it was yesterday. I picked out a dark navy-blue windowpane three-piece suit with a few custom shirts. I anxiously waited for my first order to arrive. Mark finally called to informed me that the clothes had come. I couldn't wait.

This wanting to dress my very best was a feeling that ignited a fire inside of me. It was priceless. Putting on that suit that day, placing those cufflinks on, buttoning up the vest, and throwing that jacket on made me feel like Superman with his cape. I was hooked, suit after suit, shirt after shirt, I couldn't stop. I wanted more and more. Mark recalls after working with me during those years, and the one big thing he learned from me was "To create something exceptional, your mindset must be relentlessly focused on the smallest detail."

I was meticulous, even back then, with every detail, and I am sure it drove him crazy sometimes. I began ordering more and more custom-made clothing from Mark. I was experimenting with fit, flair, and how I looked. Until you have a bespoke suit and shirt that's made to your exact shape, you have no idea how comfortable a suit can be. I started realizing that other successful people who also wore suits and understood how to dress properly, connected with me differently. Some people around town started to call me the "Three-Piece King." It was a nickname given to me by a good friend, Atlanta's own Kenny Burns, an entertainment industry executive, television, and radio host.

Not only was I having great success in real estate, but because of my newfound status as a sharp-dressed man, I had the opportunity to meet a lot of businessmen and celebrities in Atlanta's music scene. As most young men, I enjoyed being out at the club and was often found in the VIP section, wearing my customary three-piece suit, rocking out, and having a blast. Rappers and producers would walk up chuckling asking who the hell is this guy in a three-piece suit? It became who I was, my identity, which remains true to this day.

My style has continued to evolve. I have learned so much from my trips to Paris and Italy. I even have had the pleasure of having a bespoke fitting from the famous Savile Row at Kilgour's, a legendary tailor of its time, established in 1882. While I am grateful for all the beautiful garments that I've had the opportunity to wear, I am still searching for the perfect suit and the perfect fit. It's a never-ending quest for me. As my style evolves, I have created my own set of rules and my attention to detail has only gotten better.

"Manifestation is real. What you wear, how you act, and what you do in today's society matters!"

Carlo Brandelli, Kilgour Creative Director from 2003 to 2009 once said. "Bespoke is the launch pad. It is the measure of quality and excellence from which everything else follows."[1] I agree with that one-hundred percent.

Don't just take my word. Recent academic research backs up the view that wearing a suit enhances your ability to succeed in business. Psychologists at California State University at Northridge, put subjects through a series of experiments to gauge the relationship between clothes and cogency. Experiments showed that when a subject dressed formally, they were more adept at "abstract processing" – meaning they are more likely to see the big picture rather than obsess over minor details. Abstract thinking is useful when solving problems and a key attribute for entrepreneurs. Researchers say abstract thinking is helpful when hearing criticism, as the thinker can take a step back from the negative feedback rather than letting it affect their self-esteem. "Putting on formal clothes makes us feel powerful, and that changes the basic way we see the world," says Abraham Rutchick,[2] one of the authors. Michael Slepian, another of the paper's authors and a professor at Columbia Business School, believes that putting on a suit has a positive impact on our ability to see the big picture. I agree wholeheartedly with this. In fact, it's my way of life, "Kingsway"!

VII. MAKE ROOM FOR OPPORTUNITY

It was Friday night, October 25, 2002 and I was the promoter for the rapper 50 Cent at Stage East in East Hartford. While most twenty-three-year-olds were still contemplating their career, I was already a business hustler. 50 Cent was an emerging rap star and was about to burst into the mainstream. He was on the verge of signing for a major label and his debut album *Get Rich or Die Tryin'* would push him into the hip-hop stratosphere. In fact, I remember in-between our shows, he flew out to LA to sign that million-dollar deal with Dre and Eminem. That morning, I got out of the shower and started to get dressed. I put on Point Blank Body Armor, inserted an extra blade-proof Kevlar chest plate, and pressed down the velcro straps. Next, I put on a clean Russell Athletic T-Shirt, gray sweat pants, and Timberland boots. Hot-headed dudes with guns were an increasingly serious problem in Hartford. There were random shootings and regular gunshots at after-hours events.

The emerging star's act was dangerous to book. In May 2000, 50 Cent had been ambushed outside of his grandmother's house in South Jamaica's Queens borough of NYC. He was shot nine times at close range. Miraculously, he survived but suffered serious injuries to his jaw.

It was thirty dollars per ticket, with the doors opening at 9:00 p.m. Stage East was a former movie theater built in the 1940s, and had a maximum legal capacity to hold 655 people. That didn't matter however, as we had about 1,000 inside and few hundred outside trying to get in. Security was tight. I had several large men lined up in front of the stage. Before the show, security was trying to keep the fans off the stage.

After midnight, my security grabbed me to tell me that 50 Cent was here with his entourage. This was our second show together.

"Noyze you ready?" said 50 with his famous grin. "Let's do this."

"Noyze" is what everyone called me back then. Moments later, the place erupted, cheering, as 50 Cent came out on stage rapping. The whole place was shaking with energy.

It was pure adrenaline and for fifteen glorious minutes, the place was smoking like a vintage Habana cigar. Unfortunately, this vibe was about to be put out too quickly! 50 ends the song and is about to introduce another when it happens. Boooom!

There was a crack like a gunshot. It echoed around the hall. Everyone at the front rushed aside. It was a frenzy, a human stampede of raw fear as guys hit the deck. In that initial moment, I presumed it was a shooter. In a blur from the DJ booth, I saw the security guard crumple to the floor. No bullet was shot though – a champagne bottle was flung up by some disgruntled guy who had been removed from the stage earlier by that same security guard.

Soon enough it was over, but some people had been hurt. It was most certainly due to the human stampede I had witnessed. Blood was on the floor, panic in the air. As I said, it was a violent place.

Here's a lesson. I could have gone home. I should have gone home and waited till the heat died down. However, I felt I had the responsibility to check on everyone, after all it was my show. At approximately 2:00 a.m., I drove over to the Crowne Plaza Hotel in Hartford, where 50 was staying. Members of his entourage who were milling about the lobby greeted me on my arrival. They turned and acknowledged my arrival.

"You, shouldna' come back here, man. You shouldna' be in here," growls one of the G-Soldiers, (that is what his posse called themselves, a takeaway from the "G-Unit" brand 50 Cent had founded). "The boss wants to see you upstairs."

I went upstairs to the top-floor suite. "Is he OK? Is the guy all right?" I asked. 50's manager was unhappy and angry. He jabbed his finger into my chest. "It's not cool man. You screwed up, man. We need another $10,000 or you're gonna be screwed up too."

I felt the heat. This was a dangerous place for me. But I felt a growing sense of outrage at this.

"Messed up? That's his job. He manhandles a guy off the stage aggressively and the guy retaliates. This is not my fault. Here's your cash. Here's a couple of grand for the security guy. Let's just call it quits," as I peel out the cash.

Clearly it was a shake down. My intentions were to just check on him to make sure he was okay and this wasn't turning out the way I thought it would.

It was time for me to go. I turned around, left the room, and headed downstairs. All these G-Soldiers were still in the lobby, still pumped-up and with the authority to give me a beating if necessary. I probably could have been beaten to death. I brushed aside one of the soldiers on the way to the door, and I said to him, "This is bull*** man. I came back to see how your man is and this is the way you f'ing treat me!"

One of the G-Soldiers, David, who later on became a good friend of mine, told me years later that the team was amazed. "That's one brave cocky little white boy," they all agreed. I also learned from David that everyone had the code to kick me until I was dead. But my ballsy outburst had earned me a reprieve – and grudging respect. "You've got some balls to come into a place with thirty guys and start shouting."

I ended up leaving the hotel, we had another show coming up and didn't want a few bucks or issues stopping the long-term play here. We did another show with 50 Cent, G-Unit's Lloyd Banks, and Tony Yayo, along with Obie Trice at the Expo Center a few weeks later. The show was a gigantic success and to this day it was my biggest show with more than 7,500 people in attendance. We all gathered in the hotel that evening before the show on December 27, 2002 snapping memorable pictures of 50, G-Unit, and myself. I saw the security guard and told him that I was sorry that the last show went sideways. "Noyze. It wasn't your fault. It is what it is."

When I think back to where I have come from, it is moments like these that brought me one step closer to where I am today. I learned a lot about myself. I was young and headstrong. But I always wanted to sort out bad situations and do the right thing. Yes, it was chaos that night. But somehow, I felt it was my responsibility to fix it. This episode, among others, caused a shift in my life. One thing always leads to the next, though we may not realize it.

In November 2003, I was in New York City. I had my office at 114 East 32nd Street between Park and Lexington. I would travel between Hartford and New York City every day. I had a thriving digital design company where we worked with some of the biggest names in music. My driver Mario, an older man who always was dressed in a black suit, skinny tie and driver's hat, who kept his used car clean and shiny, would pick me up. I can still recall the polished leather backseat with the tinted windows. I had an early BlackBerry, the blue one with the side scroll and was always answering emails and calls while he weaved through the uptown traffic.

That day, I was on my way to meet with Jeff Robinson who was managing Alicia Keys. We had done a lot of work for his company, MBK, and we were discussing upcoming projects. Jeff was always so kind and humble despite the great success he was having with Alicia. Later that afternoon, I had meetings at Violator Records where Chris Lighty (may he rest in peace) and Mona Scott had built a powerhouse. I loved chatting with Mona; she was confident, knew what she wanted, and was always kind and sweet. We worked with her team on some of their designs, websites, and marketing materials for artists like 50 Cent, G-Unit, Clipse, Busta, and Missy Elliott. My company was originally set up as a way for me to save on marketing materials as a concert promoter. Between my shows and nightclub, this was a second income stream and a great networking business. We even started to handle the album covers for Don Omar, who was a talented Puerto Rican reggaeton singer just as the reggaeton movement was gaining attention. This was a time when flyers, posters, and promotional material were big business.

Mario pulled the car up outside Houston's restaurant on Park Avenue. I headed in to meet my attorney, Kendall Minter. He was an established entertainment lawyer, always busy but we had a special bond. His advice and feedback were always welcome. The restaurant was alive with gossip, it was like a scene out of *Sex and the City*, with its tables all filled with men in suits and their expense account clients. I was greeted nonchalantly by the head waiter, then whisked to a table where Kendall was reading *The New York Times*.

"Hey, CK, how are you?" as he folded the newspaper and placed it on the table. I first met Kendall, a graduate from Cornell University Law School in 2002. He was referred to me by my CPA at that time. He is an influential music lawyer steeped in the world of jazz and R&B representing clients like Jermaine Dupri, Lenny White, Shabba Ranks, Kool & The Gang, and Kirk Franklin to name a few. Despite our twenty-year age gap, Kendall had become a friend and to this day is like an older brother to me and still one of my attorneys.

"Man, I'm feeling good today, and it is great to see you," I said as I slid into the booth. Moments later, we settled in with a couple of glasses of Napa Cabernet Sauvignon discussing the basketball season and the merits of the new Jay-Z *Black* album. Kendall was helping with all my legal work: from setting up businesses to entertainment contract work in both Connecticut and New York. He was working on Park Avenue with a boutique law firm Rudolph & Beer, set up by Bronx-born Larry Rudolph in 1993. After all his success as an attorney, Larry went on to quit his law practice to become Britney Spears's manager.

I settled on Houston's famous hamburger with french fries, while Kendall had his favorite black-bean burger. Chief Executive George Biel opened the restaurant in 1977, and it was Kendall's go-to place for lunch. His fancy Manhattan office was across the street. This was his usual spot for meeting his friends and clients. It was now time for me to tell Kendall what I wanted to talk about. While I had been successful as a promoter, the life was not without its share of drama and dangers. The novelty of potentially getting shot was getting old, and I felt that I was ready for yet another change.

It had taken its toll on me mentally. I craved a different vibe where I could grow into a distinguished businessman, and not have to deal with the trouble and fights in my club. It also happened to be just a week after I had experienced a dear friend being stabbed over eight times. He almost died in my arms waiting for the ambulance. It was time for me to take my life to a higher level. I knew I could no longer do this. I asked Kendall what he thought about making a move to Atlanta. I had a few friends already making a small fortune in real estate down there. I knew he had just set up an office in the city. I was young, hungry, and eager to learn.

Kendall listened. I could see he was giving my situation serious consideration. In 1995, he had relocated to Atlanta where he specialized in entertainment, media matters, and sports, including handling contracts for former world boxing heavyweight champions, Ray Mercer and Evander Holyfield. He split his time between New York and Atlanta.

I wanted to get into real estate. I wanted a change of pace where the weather was better too. I wanted a way to reinvent myself and get a fresh start.

Atlanta, the major southern metropolis in Georgia, is rich with America's history and heritage. As a pivotal battleground in the American Civil War, the city had been burned to the ground by retreating Union soldiers. It was also on display during the civil rights movement in the 1960s, when the world was introduced to a young and fiery preacher by the name of Martin Luther King Jr. It has and continues to be the industrial and financial center of The South, home to Coca-Cola, then Delta Airlines, UPS, and Home Depot. The city is a center for film and television too – home to Ted Turner's Cable News Network (CNN). It has that intoxicating blend of urban culture, money, music, and media.

Atlanta had a lot of potential for upward growth at the time, and I thought that real estate was the right play. What I loved about real estate was that the cards were face up. Everything is disclosed and nothing is hidden when it comes to costs and profits. I also knew from occasionally flicking through Forbes magazine, that most of the top billionaires in the world were one way or another involved in real estate. It felt like the right move. Without any higher education or deep knowledge of how real estate worked, I realized that I had to start at the bottom.

As we finished our espresso after lunch, Minter was encouraging, "Look, I know you want to find new opportunities and find fertile ground outside of the music industry. You know, a little New York money goes a long way in Atlanta." That single sentence instantly set off the idea in my head. I made my mind up to move and move fast.

It's important to remember, there's never going to be an ideal time to do anything. You're never going to be at exactly the right place and at the right time to make a move. You can always talk yourself out of anything and everything, as most people do. You can always find excuses. There are so many people that I know who are still stuck in the same place doing the same old things. Even now they may tell me they want to make a move, while not doing anything about it. Life is short. Do it now; tomorrow is never promised.

Within the first few hours of arriving, I was blown away by the springtime heat and the new scene. This place was so cool. I had been in provincial Connecticut and cosmopolitan New York my whole life, and this was so different. Atlanta was an up-and-coming city, recovering after the dot-com boom and bust of the early 2000s, and the property market was on "roids." President George W. Bush proclaimed that America was now an "ownership society" with everyone across the nation having the opportunity to own their own place. There were government programs with the Federal Housing Administration, offering low-interest mortgages, and Fannie Mae and Freddie Mac, guaranteeing loans to first-time buyers, helping turn more low-income folks into homeowners. The real estate market in Georgia's urban metropolitan areas was on fire. The only problem was that I was short of money when I drove down to Atlanta.

How did I prepare myself for all that I wanted to do without the bank account to do it with? What I did when I arrived still holds true today in my business life. I'm certain it will work out; I have the faith and self-belief. Another strategy that works for me is to draw a list. Actually, I create several lists. It sounds so simple. Every day I look at my lists, tick off what has been achieved, and updated it with new tasks. Your list doesn't have to be pretty. Mine are sometimes scribbled on the back of envelopes or on my white linen cards. To this day, I'm always scribbling and drawing on tons of paper throughout my home office. So, now back to Atlanta, and my list toward conquering the market (I told you that I don't do anything small!). The first thing was to pick up some reading. I went to a local Borders bookstore and bought a pile of books, including: *The Millionaire Real Estate Investor*,[1] (with its come-on tagline "Anyone Can Do It ... Not Everyone Will ... Will You?"), *The Complete Guide to Flipping Properties*,[2] and the one I used to stoke up my ideas, *How to Create Multiple Stream of Income: Buying Homes in Nice Areas with Nothing Down!*[3]

The books gave me valuable resources; the handy charts helped to plot income and expenditure, and offered me information about taxation. The key for me was to learn how to sell a flipped property as quickly as possible. I underlined specific lessons to keep in mind: *Do as much of the work yourself to keep the costs down, and buy the best that your budget allows.* If you are taking on something new, ask a simple question and jot down the answer: *What do I need by way of knowledge, by way of tools, by way of information to do this job?*

I enrolled in a real estate agent class too. I wasn't planning on being an agent though, I had different plans. On the first day of class, the teacher went around asking everybody to introduce themselves. Most attendees were from real estate firms, where they would embark in future careers as agents. When it came to my turn, I stood up and declared I wasn't with any real estate firm and, furthermore, had no intention of undertaking the formal exam at the end of the course. I was going to be an investor and a developer. All I wanted was to know the required practical things, and what an agent needs to know, so that I could be educated as I had never even bought a property before. For me, it was about immersing myself in everything I could to learn about real estate. I could see half the class smirking, smiling and thinking, "Who is this guy?"

Next on the list was to set up my real estate company in Atlanta. Kendall was handling that for me. My new business adventure had just begun. I also worked part-time as a salesman. I was never afraid to work a regular job to give me enough income to allow me to focus on my dream. I started working in Rooms To Go, a national furniture store, with its Buckhead branch on Peachtree Road. I didn't like working as a showroom salesman and began to dread working for other people. In fact, I hated going. However, this was a means to an end, and it drove me. You see, I had no one to fall back on, I had responsibilities and bills. Sometimes we have to work a position we might not like while we build our business in our spare time. Dreading this job allowed me to work faster and harder in order to get the real estate business going. At night after work, on weekends, and whenever I had time off, I was planning those first tentative steps toward my real estate empire.

The more I learned, the more excited I got. Soon enough, I was ready to venture into real estate. I handed in my notice. Like the release of a caged bird, I was ready to fly.

VIII. DON'T STOP UNTIL THE JOB'S DONE

Let me step back a bit here to tell you something about my attitude in getting things done. It had been another crazy night at my nightclub in the late fall of 2004. My staff was clearing up the bottles, cans, and other trash after a show. It was nearly 3:00 a.m. and the Hartford venue was empty. We were all desperate to get home to our beds. One of my employees came downstairs to my office while I was doing the nightly paperwork. He said that the guys were unwilling to clean up the bathroom and that I should come upstairs and see for myself. "The men's room is a terrible mess. I just can't face it, man!" I was told as I walked up to them.

Never ask someone to do something you are not prepared to do yourself. When I opened the door, the stench nearly knocked me over. Someone had vomited multiple times all over the place. It was covering the floors, the sinks, it was even on the walls and mirrors. It was everywhere.

"What the ..." I muttered, as the others backed away covering their face and nose with their hands.

"Can you get me a bucket with some boiling hot water, bleach, and soap?" I asked grimacing. While I waited, I rolled up my sleeves, and told the entire staff to stand there while I cleaned the God-awful mess. For the next ten minutes, I mopped and cleaned, flushing the toilets, and then rinsing the whole place with disinfectant. I wiped down the mirrors and cleaned every part of the faucets, I then made sure the floor was spotless. I handed the mop to one of the guys.

"I'd never ask you to do anything I wouldn't be prepared to do myself. You can see how neat and clean this

is now. I want it like this every night. I don't care what kind of a mess is made. Just get it done next time." Of course, this was a nightclub, it happened again. However, I never had an issue with the staff dealing with it. Too many people in life and in business, talk the talk, but don't walk the walk. One of my favorite sayings speaks to this. *They talk right, but walk left.* By that I mean, people say they will do something, but don't ever deliver.

My mindset is: *Never stop until the job is done.* It's about having a sense of pride in anything and everything you do. My life has had ups and downs, I've had many jobs and tasks and no matter what, I've taken pride in them and got it done.

How you Do Anything is How you Do Everything

That's the attitude I took with me when I came to Atlanta. Everywhere you looked, the signs were clear that buying and selling property was the way to make it big. A corporate Atlanta builder called Beazer Homes was one of the sizzling stocks on Wall Street. It was building thousands of new homes in Florida and California. They were being snatched up by home-buyers anxious to step right onto the property conveyor. Its stock price was climbing higher every day towards eighty dollars a share. Beazer was playing a dangerous game though. Not only was it building the homes, but the builder was selling them before they were completed. It was also raising billions from speculators, then lending first-time buyers' money to buy these unfinished homes. This was the stage that was set in real estate. There was serious money to be made. I walked around central Atlanta and found it a buzzing city with great bars, sizzling clubs, stylish restaurants, and plenty of fashionable clothing stores. I smelled opportunity, the same way I did later on when I moved to California.

I needed to be near where the "action" was happening. I wrote a check and moved into an apartment on Lenox Road in Buckhead, which houses the city's modernist skyscrapers and iconic towers.

I searched for the perfect opening investment, and it wasn't long before I stumbled upon my first property. The home was in Atlanta's Fulton County. It was for sale for $80,000, but with hard work, it could be worth a great deal more. It wasn't a huge renovation, but it proved to be a successful one. The sellers were Dooley & Jan Properties who had bought it for $66,900 in March. The Bank of New York CWBS (Country Wide Asset Backed Securities Inc.) had paid $113,850 in March the previous year. This suggested a foreclosure, so it had significantly dipped in value and was unoccupied. The house, which was in the south-west of the city, was in decent condition compared to some neighboring properties which were dilapidated. It was built in 1946 after World War Two for one of the many GIs and their families who were returning to start their lives in Atlanta's suburbs. It was a detached brick and clapperboard home with two mature trees shading the front window and porch. While it had six rooms, the next-door properties were considerably larger. It wasn't a huge renovation. It was a small house; soon I would undertake much bigger development projects. This was the first deal and my starting point.

By May 2006, I had managed to save $3,000, which I would use as a security deposit to buy the home. It was nearly all I had. I didn't have sufficient credit to get a full mortgage – and without a track record, despite approaching plenty of banks, they were simply not interested. With forty-eight hours left before the deadline for closing the deal, I was still without the mortgage money. Unless I found a solution, I would even lose my earnest money. I was scouring the newspaper and saw an advertisement for "Hard Money Loans" from StreetSmart. It gave me goosebumps. I had nothing to lose, so I called them up and spoke to a guy named Sam, who was friendly and receptive. I was honest and polite and told him about my deal and what I wanted to do. The call went smoothly. He told me StreetSmart knew the area and were very interested in the property and the deal. I explained my deadline. "Sure, we're very interested in what you're doing. Let me get back later today after I have spoken to our approval team." I responded, "That's great, I'll be waiting for your call."

In what seemed to be like days, I finally received a call back. "Chris, it's Sam. We like the deal, and we can close tomorrow," he told me. By the end of the next day I had closed the deal and got the loan, including the construction budget to fix the property. Sam explained to me how the private money lending worked.

"Okay, your loan is for three months."

These were designed for real estate secured loans, so that investors like me could use it to purchase a property, then flip it. "And another thing, all your earnest money is non-refundable. It's $1,000 for properties under $100,000, and $2,000 for properties over $100,000, so you need a grand for us," said Sam.

It was all remarkably clear and simple. I was given $80,000 to buy the property. They were also allowing $25,000 for further construction work. The total loan was for $103,000. It was expected that the property would be worth somewhere between $150,000 to $160,000 after all completed work. This was a great potential profit, but it was never guaranteed. I signed the deal, said goodbye to the furniture store and became a full-time, fledgling real estate entrepreneur.

In truth, I didn't really know how it all worked. Upon completion of the work, they told me they would come, inspect it, and then reimburse me for it. Yet, there was still another problem to figure out. I didn't even have the extra money to start the construction work. I had to come up with a solution. What if I undertook the demolition work myself and used the allowance to hire the necessary contractors for the other jobs? I made a rough calculation and estimated the demolition budget to be $8,000. While I didn't have money to pay for other workers to start the construction, once the demolition work was inspected, I would be able to draw a check against my construction budget, and use the $8,000 to hire contractors and live off of it for the next few months.

I remember Sam showing up to inspect the demo to write me the check. He was laughing because he knew what I was doing. As he wrote the check and handed it to me with a grin he said, "Smart, let's see what you can do young man."

It took a few days to arrange the documentation for the sale, giving me time to draw up a blueprint and prepare a work schedule. On Friday, June 9, 2006, I was handed the house keys. The next forty-seven days would change my outlook on life forever. It was a lot of work, which I did most of it myself. During a hot and sweltering June and July in Atlanta, I began the heavy lifting labor. Not wanting to spend a nickel on demolition work done by contractors, I went to Home Depot and bought a sledge-hammer. I tackled all the heavy masonry work myself and collected the draw check for $8,000.

Over that first weekend, the news was filled with stories of impending tropical Storm Alberto, which was predicted to hit Georgia. I was oblivious to this. I arrived daily at 8:00 a.m. Immediately, I started bashing down connecting walls and door frames, ripping out the old bathroom and kitchen appliances, and taking tiles off the wall. Sure, I was a fit and strong guy, but within minutes, the sweat was dripping off my face, and my T-shirt was soaking wet. In August, the southern heat is unbearable, and I was sweating so bad that it would seep into my eyes and sting. I would swig countless bottles of water to replenish my fluids, but there was little time to admire my handiwork. My attitude was to keep going, working as hard as I could to finish the job as quickly as I could. This is something my friends now say about me all the time, especially Rob Dyrdek, calling it #kingspeed! I am always moving fast, even faster now. Time is money.

The passing neighbors looked on curiously at me. I was decked out in a T-shirt, jeans, and Timberland construction boots, working fourteen hours a day, with no days off. Thankfully, the tropical storm fizzled out before reaching Atlanta. There were at least some light showers to cool the heat wave. There were new hardwood floors to install and internal walls to rebuild. I built a new porch and stairwell, did the landscaping, improved the yard, and fixed the driveway. I hired a local electrician for the re-wiring and a plumber to install a new shower and toilet. I bought several buckets of paint and painted the internal walls, along with the brick walls outside, finishing off the new porch in fresh white paint with brown trim. I laid down new stone slabs, cutting back the weeds and grass. After I cleaned up the mess and debris, I soaked and wiped every surface to remove all of the dust, plaster, footprints, and splotches of paint from the floor. It was immaculate.

Previously, it had been a gloomy place. It was hard to see because several large bushes were overgrown, and the trees kept the house in the shade. Grooming this out-of-control foliage would make a massive difference, so I splurged an extra $1,500 on land-scapers who hacked back the bushes and planted flowers in the garden. It all helped to let in daylight into the rooms, changing the whole feel and mood of the property. I always try to imagine – again I'm visualizing – what it will look like when finished. I could picture how it would look at its best.

When I set up the real estate company, I figured the easy part would be the construction. I noticed many people were struggling to sell the property. The only way to pay off the hard money loan and make a profit was to sell that property as quickly as you could. I needed a quick return. I needed to find a way to move more properties when I got this momentum going. I knew that a lot of people were putting listings with real estate agents and not moving them, I also knew that people were putting their houses on Craigslist, a simple online classified advertising service started by Craig Newmark in San Francisco. It was where upwardly mobile urban dwellers in New York, Chicago, and California were renting apartments, finding jobs, and meeting people. I had a brilliant idea. Instead of listing these locally, why not list them in wealthier areas like New York and Chicago? My idea was to place an advertisement in those two cities to attract wealthier individuals to invest in the property. They could get more properties for their same investment locally here in Atlanta and spread out money across multiple homes for that same investment in Chicago or New York. I pitched the investment idea and the house at $170,000. It worked. A young guy from Chicago called me. We spoke on the phone, and he flew down. He loved the place and bought it as part to his investment portfolio for $168,000.

On Wednesday, July 26, 2006, I took a shower and put on my suit – for the first time in several weeks – and walked back into Sam's office. "Wow, Chris," Sam said as he stepped up from his desk. "What?" I replied.

"Most people never close the deals this fast, we are very impressed."

Three days later, I got my check for the profits from the deal, which was $65,676.40. These were my profits and earnings for forty-five days of work. I headed to the Peachtree Mall and bought a couple of suits and shirts; I then reinvested the rest back into my business. It was such an exciting feeling. I came down with nothing, and now I had $65,676 in the bank. My real estate empire was just beginning.

In reality, when I look back on the heydays of my real estate business, I was what you would describe as a workaholic. I was up at 4:30 a.m. and then went to bed by 11:00 p.m. Life was work, work, work, and more work. I was fatigued and exhausted most of the time. Sure, in the short term, it paid dividends for me, but it wasn't a sustainable thing to do for the future.

When I closed that first deal, Sam at StreetSmart was astonished by my quick execution.

"Do you want another property?"

"I want three more properties," I replied.

Sam smiled and nodded. I bought three more properties from the real estate company with the profits. One of the properties was a large multi-acre lot that I wanted to develop; the two other properties I knew I could also flip quickly. The hard money guys loved me. Every time I got a property, I was in and out of it in record time, always staying within the budget. Soon, I was getting the deals without even requiring an earnest deposit. I was building this great relationship. We did things the right way, which was how we ended up surviving so much longer than anyone else. They were giving me the properties and signing the deal, because I was doing what I said I would.

I learned ways to work smarter. This was about building a team and embracing the right people. You always have to build the right team, which I will get into in a few chapters. I had proven to myself that I could learn quickly and practically.

SECTION II: THE SET BACK

IX. LET FAILURE BE YOUR FUEL

Positive energy is vital to me. Some people have been slowly drowning in a metaphorical Sargasso Sea of negativity, which is taking away their hope. I recognize how tough it is for millions of people looking for a break. I was that same kid. No money, no credit, no wealthy family members to bail me out, and feeling like there was no way out. I have a deep respect and admiration for anyone who has made it the hard way. I have a strong belief that the American Dream still exists for those who are prepared to work for it, and who align themselves with the right energy. What still makes our nation great is the ability for anyone, no matter what the circumstances, to pull themselves up – with a combination of determination, hard work, human decency, and a little bit of good fortune. I'm not naïve though. I understand why a fear of failure prevents people from even starting out on the journey.

I've talked about the boom and bust in Atlanta and my arrival in LA. Let me give you some more background about my journey and how I got up again after one of my darkest days. I overcame this time by positive thinking, my will to never quit, and the love of friends who supported me when it mattered most.

Let me rewind to late September 2008. My alarm on my iPhone went off at 5:00 a.m. I eased myself out of bed and switched on the television. I made myself an espresso, had breakfast, showered, and dressed as usual to go into the office. My day started like any other day. Everything was seemingly normal, until the early news bulletin started reporting on the imminent collapse of one of America's towering financial houses. At first the information was patchy and seemed spurious even.

"We understand a major announcement is to be made about the future of an unnamed Wall Street institution," reported a blonde-haired newscaster on Fox Business News.

"Sources say that they may be about to collapse. But this is unconfirmed at this stage. We will keep you informed. Stay tuned!"

I was curious but unfazed as I headed to my office on Peachtree Street. Coming through the lobby, I could sense the magnitude of this breaking financial story. The television screens were now confirming a major collapse, and the New York Stock Exchange was spooked. There was red blood all over the stock charts. I was now awakened by the wider implications, and my brain ran the gamut of emotions.

When I stepped out of the elevator on the thirty-third floor into the lobby, I felt a strange shiver run down my spine. I turned the corner and walked into my office. Ray was already there. He had a serious look and was deeply concerned.

"What's up?" I asked.

"It's the mortgage company, bro."

"What about them?"

"They ain't doin' any more loans."

"What do you mean? We've got five houses ready to go this week."

"They're not playing ball," he said.

"Oh, crap."

It was September 26, 2008, and my world was about to get flipped upside down. I picked up the phone and tried to get through to our lenders. The phone just rang out. I tried again and again. When I got through, it went to a voicemail.

"We're sorry that no-one can answer your call right now. Please try later." Our company had five properties in the pipeline, ready to be closed with signed deals. We had a dozen of them with pending construction due to begin, however, there was no funding available. Without warning, the game had changed. If it wasn't your primary residence with an 827 credit score and twenty percent down, the real estate loan companies were not in the game. We weren't going to sell the houses because we couldn't get our investors a loan. We had many properties in mid-construction, with teams of plumbers, electricians, and general builders, all employed by us. We had such success that we also owned our own construction company. Everyone was awaiting further instructions.

"Stand the guys down for the rest of the day, until we see how this pans out," I instructed.

Ray made a call to the foreman, and the teams were sent home – many unaware that it would turn out to be longer than expected. The FICO system ran the range from poor-quality and risk at 300, to sure-fire safe 850. The Fair, Isaac and Company was the benchmark for loans, and anything over 800 was solid. Anyone and everyone in the real estate market was hit. I mean everyone, developers, home-builders, or construction firms, and even agents. As the day went on and the full gravity of the collapse emerged, more dominos began to fall quickly. This wasn't confined to the United States either. Banks in the UK, the rest of Europe, including Spain, Ireland, Italy, and France were feeling the crunch. Even the tiny Atlantic island of Iceland was experiencing the crash. Everyone was in a frenzy. It was an absolute mess.

For thirty minutes, I sat in my chair, staring out the window over downtown Atlanta with its magnificent skyline. I wondered what we could do. In those initial hours, we hit the phones. Ray, the team, and I wanted to have a clear understanding of what was happening. We both knew it was over. It had imploded so quickly. Six months earlier, we had been on a whirlwind tour with investors in Houston,

Dallas, and Chicago. During this time, I remember being on the fifty-third story of the Chase Tower, with spectacular views over Lake Michigan and the rest of the Chicago skyline. Ray and I were preparing to present to other investors. They were referrals to bring them into our portfolio. We were constantly bringing in new clients and investors to look at our properties. This was just another typical day. We had expanded the business into Chicago and Houston, and we were in full motion. The momentum was full-speed, and we thought it would never change.

CDOs. Up until this point I had never heard of them and yet, these three letters came to represent the most massive investment boom and bust in recent history. Countless financial "experts" around the globe had never heard of them either – including some senior banking figures who ran massive financial organizations. The fabled CDO was the "collateralized debt obligation," a financial instrument perfected by the wizards at Wall Street's investment banks, such as Bear Stearns, Lehman, and Merrill Lynch, and blessed by the hapless rating agencies. It was a simple concept that became layered in complexity as each level took its share. The process began in the office of major US mortgage brokers, such as New Century Financial Corporation, Aurora, BNC Mortgage, part of Lehman, and Countrywide. They would lend, finance, and provide capital for houses purchased. They had to borrow the money first though from proper banks, because they didn't have the money. So right across the US, a host of creative companies sprang up such as OwnIt Mortgage, LowerMyPayment.com, Deep Green Financial, Sea Breeze Financial Services, and Mortgage Warehouse. These guys were putting together packages of mortgages for up to 1,000 homes, so they could continue to sell them on to one of the Wall Street banks. They would buy up blocks of homes. They would then arrange a deal to sell to Lehman with the property deeds to be used as collateral. In the housing boom, when everyone paid their monthly payments, it was a license to print money. All Lehman did was buy the loans and create a bond which was then called "securitizing the debt." This was a security that could then be sold to other investors around the globe. Because it had Lehman's name on it and it was invariably given a top score by the three leading credit-rating companies, such as Standard & Poor's, Fitch, and Moody's, they sold like proverbial hot cakes. These CDOs were called "mortgaged backed securities" and our idea was to get in and start building our own portfolio of properties and sell big blocks of them like the major banks were doing. All our investors, especially the investors at the Chicago meeting were keen to understand what we were doing.

I had done my homework and had seen that California, Florida, Nevada, and parts of the mid-west centered around Chicago had reached saturation point for CDOs, and Atlanta presented an untapped potential. These were guys who were already looking to invest. Chicago was a totally different type of market where the value was higher. In Atlanta, they could get more properties for their dollars. They were as motivated as we were. It was the days when everyone believed they had the Midas touch. We all thought this would never end. Well, not quite all of us. One evening several months before the crash, Mark my tailor, (the one that I have spoken of earlier) and I got together to catch up at Nickiemoto's, an Asian café and sushi bar in Midtown, famed for its outré Drag-a-Maki show directed by Martina Diamante.

"How is it going?" he asked me as we sipped cocktails in the bar.

"Really well. Too good to be true," I replied.

Mark lowered his voice to a whisper and spoke about one of his mysterious clients, an ultra-wealthy, old-money American billionaire who never sought publicity.

"I was speaking to my oldest customer, when I told him about you and how you were still buying property in the US. He asked me if I thought you were crazy. He said that his business partner bought a Gulfstream G550 with no money down and because of this he knew the real estate bubble was about to burst. His advice was to tell you to sell everything you have in real estate now – and get the hell out of it."

"Come on. That's crazy, Mark. We're making money. What does he mean get out of real estate? We're selling every property we can flip right now."

"He told me to tell you to get everything out of real estate in the United States. Do not invest another dollar and get out of it."

Four months later the crisis happened – and the market crashed. When he said, "Get out!" We bought more. We were closing them left and right, closing three to four properties on a Thursday, then taking off to Miami for the weekend. Life was amazing. We saw no signs of why we should stop, let alone take advice from someone we had never met.

Now, as I sat staring out on the skyline, the other big news was the collapsing of Wachovia Bank, based in Charlotte, North Carolina. It was one of the biggest local mortgage lenders in the US and was in deep trouble too. It was bought by Wells Fargo on October 3, 2008. On Monday, October 6, the whole world began to unravel as a series of larger seismic shocks emanated from the financial earthquake. Bigger than me, other more established real estate players, such as Stan Thomas, John Wieland, Wayne Mason, and Ben Carter all felt the draught. While this did not impact our real estate company directly, it meant the whole market grounded to a halt. The scramble caused our ever-decreasing pockets of cash to pay off each bill as it hit our desks.

Even the glitzy W Atlanta-Downtown hotel, with its well-heeled condos was in deep trouble. Somehow our real estate company managed to stagger on for many months after the eventual banking collapse. I made an effort each day to dress properly for work, giving the outward impression that I was able to ride the storm. However, day after day, blows would keep on coming, as millions defaulted on their home loans. Across the United States, the situation was pretty bad. The reckless expansion of mortgage-backed investments was exposed, and thus engulfing every financial institution. The liquidity of cash had dried up and everyone was scrambling.

While around me, friends, investors, and I were taking the hit, some with intense personal implications, I never filed for bankruptcy. I was managing to scrape by, trimming over-heads, hacking back on payroll, halting my personal spending, selling a few possessions, and fighting the fires. Thinking back on it now, the smart play would have been to keep all the cash and the assets, and do what most people do, file bankruptcy. I just could not cop out like that. It was one of the most difficult times in my life. I was at rock bottom, losing it all. It was a surreal shift from the life I had, closing deals to barely scraping by. A few weeks before all of this happening, I would have been jumping on a plane down to South Beach in Miami. I would be enjoying the Sagamore penthouse, where I would wake up and have the best crab cake benedict with an English muffin on the beach. Now this was a real-life horror story, not knowing where I was going to live or how I was going to get enough money to eat. I mean, we had lost it *all*.

We paid every single debt we could. I was running around like a maniac. By mid-2009, it was a hellish nightmare. I was trying to stay positive, and I was trying to forge ahead, but there are often uncomfortable moments you cannot ignore. The darkest point of my business collapse came as I sat in my home in Chastain Park, down the street from the lush North Fulton golf course. It was the middle of the working day, and I was famished.

I was in my personal office alone and hungry, I realized that I had no money, not a cent. It was all gone. What had gone wrong? How did we not see this, and what could we have done differently? It is something that we all probably think about when times are bad. After everything was done, I was in a lease-option to purchase, a house I was going to flip, next to the golf course. And now I had nothing.

The phone rang. It was my mother.

"Hi, son. I hear it's pretty bad out there. I'm worried about you," she said to me.

I could not speak. There was a massive lump in my throat. I was holding back the tears as my mom tried to reassure me. I never had investments other than property to sell. No stocks. No bonds. No pension funds. Zero. All I had was cash in the bank, and that was pretty much gone too. I had nothing. I vowed right there and then that if I ever recovered from this – I would have savings for a rainy day and ensure that my business interests were diversified across a range of assets. That was a brutal way to learn about life. But this intense failure was like fuel on a fire. I knew two things: One, this would not last, and two, I would make it back!

It's okay to fail, it's okay to hit rock bottom, and all success stories have had a low point at some level. This is something we don't admit enough but it true. It's my ability to focus on reinvention that I believe has allowed me to come back from failures and embarrassments. It's just not okay to dwell on that failure or mistake, and let it consume your mind which will prevent you from rebuilding and growing again.

Here's how I look at this.

Life is like a series of ten doors to me. We measure our lives by a series of successes to reach our dreams or desires. We continue to get down a series of ten doors until such a time when we reach the end. That could be fifty doors or even one-hundred doors. It all depends on your dreams. But I believe that in order to get more doors opened, you have to close the ones behind you. In life, people keep doors open, and never get new opportunities to get to another level, because they continue to have those open doors. They may represent unforgiveness, lost relationships, bad decisions, failed businesses, and so on. There is too much attachment to all these open doors, that you are preventing yourself from new opportunities. You can use this analogy in so many different ways in life. We have to keep it moving and focus our mind on the future and where we are going, if you want to get there. These doors representing the past are keeping you stuck in mud. Allow these doors to close in order to fuel your future, nothing more and nothing less. I always say, "Keep it moving and don't look back."

X. DON'T EVER QUIT

This is probably one of the most important things you will ever hear. DON'T EVER QUIT! Yes, you! I can tell you that throughout my life there have been deep dark moments, times when I wanted to throw in the towel and just give up. Sadness, depression are all real battles we face with rejection, failures and mistakes. However, all the frustration, the headaches, the uncertainty, and the self-doubts are all fear-based and can play tricks on your mind. You can't let them affect you and keep you down.

A long time ago, I discovered a poem that really spoke to me, said to be written by Edgar A. Guest. I had this version framed and gave it to a friend. That friend then later in life gave it back to me during my darker days, and it still sits in my home today. During difficult times, I look at it and remind myself of those dark and challenging periods when I was able to pull myself up. I know that I am able to change the course of my life by never giving up and never quitting. It goes:

DON'T QUIT

When things go wrong, as they sometimes will,
When the road you're trudging seems all uphill,
When the funds are low and the debts are high,
And you want to smile, but you have to sigh,
When care is pressing you down a bit,
Rest if you must, but don't you quit.

Life is queer with its twists and turns,
As every one of us sometimes learns,
And many a person turns about,
When they might've won have they stuck it out.
Don't give up though the pace seems slow,
You may succeed with another blow.

Often the struggler has given up,
When he might have captured the victor's cup,
And he learned too late when the night came down,
How close he was to the golden crown.
Success is failure turned inside out,
So stick to the fight when you're hardest hit,
It's when things seem worst that you mustn't quit.

This has been a monumental and powerful piece of advice that came from a piece of paper sitting in a golden frame in my home. This is by far the truest statement – Never ever give up!

Let me share a personal story here. I was in a deteriorating financial situation after the global banking collapse. During my earlier Atlanta days, my friend Justin Anthony, a restaurant owner, was close to a personal trainer and gym owner named Dolvett Quince. He invited Dolvett over to one of my house gatherings. We hit it off instantly. We both came from Connecticut, although he had lived in Florida before moving to Atlanta. He was originally from Bridgeport. We became close friends, and I was welcomed in the gym that he owned. He was always warm and personable, with a terrific attitude and a deeply encouraging manner.

It was easy to see how he would become one of Atlanta's premier health and fitness trainers. He set up Body Sculptor, a private personal training studio with the promise of "Changing lives one rep at a time." A local radio station personality started talking about how Dolvett had changed his life, and celebrities soon began to frequent his gym. He ended up helping celebrities, athletes, and actors, among others, get in the best shape of their lives. Among them, Angela Bassett, who won a Golden Globe for her portrayal of Tina Turner, Boris Kodjoe, Nicole Ari Parker, Daniel Wilcox of the Baltimore Ravens, and singer Justin Bieber, are some of the people who were all impacted by Dolvett's training.

I was one of his regulars. Dolvett was walking the floor in the gym when I arrived. He knew I had lost it all. He knew times were really tough for me. I thought working out might help lift my mood and give me something positive to focus on. Dolvett could sense I was pretty low. After the hour-long workout, I felt so much better. I was sipping some water from a paper cup by the cooler when Dolvett put his hand in his pocket. He pulled out around $800 and handed it to me.

"King, go take care of yourself. I love you, man," he said.

"Wow! Dolvett. Nah man, I can't," I replied. But reluctantly I ended up accepting.

This generosity, at a desperate point in my life was both humbling and emotional. At such a critical junction, you really find your true friends. Moments like this give you hope about humanity. If you have a Dolvett in your life, someone willing to be there in your darkest times, cling on, and cherish them for the rest your life. They truly love you for who you are, rather than who you appear to be, or what you can do for them. In the midst of the Atlanta mayhem, Dolvett renewed my faith in human nature. Up until then, I was the one who was always generous and gave freely of my money. This was the first time I had experienced this on the receiving end. Dolvett's kindness was like a gentle spray of fuel (if there's such a thing), and it fired me up. To have someone who really cares about you like that is empowering. It made me grab ahold of my situation. I had to confront the inevitable. It encouraged me to get out and fight again.

I still couldn't pay the rent, so I phoned up the landlord to tell him about my difficulties. Honesty is always the best policy. It is never a sound plan to pretend that this isn't happening and not face the situation head-on. I encourage anybody who's ever going through hard times, to be honest and upfront and not to be embarrassed or ashamed. We are all human and make mistakes. This was about not shrinking from tough decisions. That afternoon, the landlord came around to Chastain Park. I invited him up to the house.

"Thanks for coming over. I need to tell you about my terrible situation. I've lost everything. I can't pay the rent anymore, let alone honor the lease option to buy this place," I admitted. I had high hopes for this place with a lease/purchase agreement to build it up as my next high-end flip.

"Hey, Mr. King, thank you for letting me know. Believe me, you are not in this alone. There are thousands in this awful situation. I appreciate the fact that you've told me face-to-face. Some guys are just disappearing and we can't find them," he said.

"Well. I promise to sort out everything that I can, but I'll have to hand back the keys. I owe you a month's rent and when I get back on my feet ..."

"Don't worry about that," interrupted the landlord. "If you can get out of the house in the next couple of days, don't worry about last month's rent. You were always so kind and you really kept up the property."

"I know. I loved this place."

After the landlord departed, instead of feeling deflated, I felt strangely empowered. I wrote out a priority list of what I needed to do. I counted out the remaining money. I then spent the next two days neatly packing my clothing and belongings. I arranged to have them held in storage. Then, I headed over to Ray's condo.

He quickly said, "Hey, bro, you know you are family, so whatever is ours is yours. You have always been there for me. I guess it's my turn."

"Thanks bro, I'm not really sure where to go from here but, as always, thanks for being a best friend!"

"Sure thing," he said, as he hugged me.

That night, I tried to sleep on a futon mattress in Ray's guest room, which he had converted into his home office. I knew hitting rock bottom had to happen. I accepted it. It was at that moment that I knew it couldn't get any worse. I believe this is a crucial point for anyone who hits rock bottom. There comes a point when you'll experience complete failure, an all-time low, when you have to get real with yourself. You have to accept it by owning it, because that is the only way to grow from it. By accepting it and owning it, you allow yourself to rebuild and focus on the road ahead. Some stay focused on what they had and never seem to get back on their feet. I have seen so many people not really bounce back from failures because they refuse to accept that it is happening, and get caught up in the "used-to-be's" or dwell in excuses on why it wasn't their fault and never really find their way ahead.

We can be our own worst enemies. That's where I believe faith takes over and allows you to see what's ahead. As long as you keep moving forward, you continually move away from adversity. It is always temporary; this is something I know very well.

"Remember things happen for us, not to us."

I came from humble beginnings, so what could be worse? That, to me, is an impactful statement. When you fall, you have to embrace the fact that you are falling and get back up. Hitting rock bottom in life is sometimes necessary.

As I laid down that night, I was restlessly soul-searching and finding out some harsh truths about myself. I was truly humbled. I also felt I would come back bigger and stronger than ever. I was determined not to let this defeat me. I knew sleeping on this futon mattress was not a long-term option. I needed another plan.

After several months, I moved on, started making deals, moved into my own apartment and was making some money. I was able to repay my small debt to Dolvett, even though I knew he wasn't expecting it. Several years later, he was transitioning from Atlanta to LA, becoming a celebrity trainer on NBC's top television series, *The Biggest Loser*. At this time in my life, I was in the midst of big successes. I would pick up the bill and pay for dinners in LA, remembering what he had done for me. Not that I had to, but because I wanted to. I wanted to return the favor. Never forget the people who look out for you or take care you along the way.

Dolvett had emerged as a celebrity with television success and as an author but has remained a true brother. His book, *The 3-1-2-1 Diet*, came out in November 2013 and quickly became a best-seller. In the book, Dolvett inscribed: "You've inspired me in so many areas of my life. I hope this book gives you the inspiration you need. Brothers for life." Moments like that are just the fuel I need, and I knew I was never going to quit, and eventually I ended up bouncing back!

Before jumping into this comeback story for the both of us, let me spend a little time on a very important subject to me. It's crucial to know who your real friends are. There was a moment in Dolvett's life where he too hit a rough patch, just like he was there for me, I was there for him. This is an important lesson, because fate changes so quickly. If it's not a friend helping you out, it can be a phone call, or a meeting that can change your life which is why you never quit.

After much struggle and rebuilding my business, both Dolvett and I had a few successful years, and we were dying to celebrate. The perfect evening came about. He invited me to be his table guest at a celebrity fundraiser on Thursday, December 12, 2013. With his book recently released, he was flying high in *The New York Times* best-sellers list in the run-up to Christmas. Dolvett and I were in rare form for a black-tie event at MILK studio in LA. Before the event, we met at Tom Ford on Rodeo Drive in Beverly Hills. The store is always a very special place filled with great energy. Tonight was even better than usual. We made our way to the back door where I had a regular designated space for my Rolls-Royce Phantom. After parking the car, we knocked on the back door and made our way through to the changing-room area. It was one of those occasions when everybody from the security guys to the mailroom staff were a part of the energy and genuinely enjoying the buzz. Dolvett and I were reliving the good old times in Atlanta here in the Rodeo store. We were laughing and cracking jokes and taking comical shots at each other, enjoying the usual high-end cocktails that are customary during our visits to the Beverly Hills store. While I was getting the final details sorted on my tux, Dolvett was sorting out his bow tie. The laughs kept on going, one after the other. Even Justin and Jason who have become friends were laughing and cracking jokes. It was always high energy and fun with them. The last stitch was put in place, and it was time to get dressed and go. We headed out the back door, jumped back into the Rolls and headed to the event.

After the cocktail reception, the celebrity crowd went in for dinner with a performance from Justin Timberlake. After dinner came the auction. The actor Kevin Connolly from the hit show, *Entourage*, was at our table, along with several actresses. After polishing off a few bottles of wine, which loosened us up, the auction was soon underway with actress Sharon Stone as the auctioneer. I'd had a good couple of months, so I was ready for the bidding. One of the star prizes was an Ed Ruscha painting. Ruscha is one of the legends of American Pop and Conceptual Art, influenced by Jasper Johns and others. He produced paintings, collages, and prints in the 1960s. He was also still active in the 2000s. The bidding started at $30,000.

"$31,000, over there," shouted Sharon as a hand was raised.

"Who will give me $32,000?" A second hand went up.

"Thank you, what about $33,000?" The first hand raised again.

"Who will give me $35,000?" The second bidder signaled again.

"Now, who will give us $40,000?" she encouraged.

I felt a rush to my head – but again, if you never take a risk – and raised my hand and shouted. "$37,500!"

Sharon stormed down from the stage and came right up to my table. "$37,500?" she shouted, hands on her hips. She leaned over and pulled opened my shirt to reveal a diamond necklace with a large pendant full of diamonds that I used to wear in my flashier days.

"Oh, my God. You can afford it, you cheapskate. Give me $40,000." She was smiling.

"$40,000 then," I laughed out loud.

Sharon Stone bent over, and gave me a kiss on the forehead. I ended up paying $40k for the Ruscha painting. After the auction, Sharon came over as a photographer snapped our shots. We kept cracking up and joking about how much fun we had. It was a great cause, and more importantly, a lot of money was raised. Personally, it was one of those evenings with the right kind of energy that provided memories that would last a lifetime. Not to mention an Ed Ruscha was a great investment piece that ended up going up in value. I always found it smart for charities to auction off art. It not only raises great money for the charity but the person buying it gains something of value to remember and hold on to.

It's moments like that with Dolvett that reminds me of how we didn't quit, we didn't give up. We both had up and downs but we kept it moving. It reminds me of another moment that was surreal.

Anytime I hear someone talk about jets or private planes, I'm always a bit incredulous that I get to charter those. Remember? I'm still that kid from Hartford with the used car trying to make it, and I have never quit and never stopped believing in myself. I never allowed my circumstances to dictate my future, or even worse, allowed my current position to stop me from thinking and dreaming big. I have designed many vision boards in my life, including the ones I have today: with properties around the world, a list of accomplishments, and wedding images in Italy and –Yes, I want to be married again if I can find true love. The vision board also features vineyards and family gatherings. These are very different from the vision boards I first made. There is nothing wrong with the ones of the past. They were mostly material items that I ended up manifesting to coming true. I remember distinctly building one with a Learjet and many other material items. There are instances when it is hard to fathom what's happened in my life. Many years ago, I was asked to be the cover story of *Executive and VIP Aviation International,* an exclusive magazine devoted to private jet enthusiasts. I was being interviewed by Margie Goldsmith, a well-respected and award-winning New York-based journalist. Here I was pulling up to Van Nuys airport, one of the busiest business airports of the United States and also in the heart of the San Fernando Valley. This international hub airstrip isn't as well-known as LAX, but it is one of the most active, with its clientele of celebrities, film and rock stars, and business executives landing in Los Angeles.

At Van Nuys, I am a regular customer of BJETS, owned by Michael Babil, a recognized leader in private aviation. He is also a great friend of mine. His business philosophy makes me comfortable and at ease, so it's no wonder he has a long list of exclusive clients.

As I got comfortable on-board one of my favorite planes, the Gulfstream 450 for our chat, Margie asked me a bunch of questions for the publication. Meeno, of course, was hired for the shoot on my recommendation, and there we were shooting away. As always, we created wonderful images together, and alongside the written part of the article, it was a truly great piece. Such moments remind me to never to quit, that anything is possible. No matter what past mistakes are made, there is always tomorrow.

XI. DON'T LET OTHERS DRAIN YOU DRY

Negative energy is such a waste. I don't like being around people who exhibit this draining quality. I know I sound harsh, but I refuse to even be around them. My advice for you: Stay clear of these individuals, they simply suck out all of your drive. They can also be dream killers, reflecting their fears or bad energy on you. If I'm in a room and the energy is off balance – I'm the guy to get up and walk out. Recently, I was at Nobu in West Hollywood for a casual dinner with my good friends Bill and Jennifer. We all had a long week and had been looking forward to a relaxing dinner to catch up. Everything in this West Hollywood restaurant was on point. The setting was perfect. The vibe was chill. Our corner table, where I like to sit, was set out immaculately. The Kanpachi sashimi was exquisite as always. The atmosphere began to change, as the restaurant filled up and got busier. Ever so slightly, the energy began to shift. It was tiny things to begin with. There were excessively noisy people at the next table. Their cursing and loud behavior along with throwaway comments might have been funny at first, but it began to infringe on our experience. I found it overbearing and unnecessary. This impacted our table. Should we move? One friend thought that we should just ignore it, while others felt it was interfering with our enjoyment. What happened next was unfortunate and yet unavoidable from my perspective. I took my napkin from my lap, left the unfinished food on my plate, and called over the waiter for the bill. I didn't make a scene, but it was essential for me to move on. Why would we want to be distracted in a high-end restaurant by immature diners who, though they have money, absence of class and common sense? It was a downright lack of respect for others. Some people can't just be in the moment and truly enjoy themselves, they need to be rowdy and loud. They are attention seekers. Successful people don't need to do this. This seems to be a common thing nowadays, online and in everyday life, and yet it is happening far too often in our society.

"Focus on what you believe and it will come to fruition."

This reminds me of when we set up the landscaping business; it didn't have the longevity we would have liked. Because of it, we were mocked for our failings. Indeed, we were ridiculed. There was a point after the business had failed when some family and "friends" would tell me, "Go and get a regular job, you loser!"

"What were you three thinking, I told you it wouldn't work!"

I had the guts and fearlessness to try and make an effort to start something of my own. It takes courage and guts to attempt to build your life from nothing. I was being laughed at for doing my own thing and for not taking the more conventional route of getting a job somewhere safe. There is nothing wrong with this. A lot of people are living a great life, doing just that. It just wasn't for me. It is my belief that nothing great in life is accomplished by playing it safe. And think about it, no "safe" job is ever really safe. Anything can happen at any time and change your circumstances, no matter how secure you may think it is. However, that abuse from family and friends was still present in the back of my mind. It made me sick. It's much easier to look forlornly at the pretty girl from a distance, rather than get out on the dance floor and ask her to dance. Here's the thing to remember. *You don't need to listen to what anyone else has to say about your life.* It's your life! You decide! You have options in your life, and you don't need anyone but yourself to make up that choice.

Even our closest family members, who truly love us, can be our biggest dream-killers, and they don't even know it. Family members or close friends may be unhappy or even jealous, so even though they surely love you, it's instinctive. Some people just don't want to see others being successful, or they want to see you successful just not more successful than them. That's why a lot of people spend more time ridiculing and making fun on the side, rather than actually getting out there on that dance floor to make it happen. Another one of my favorite quotes is, "Family and friends won't start supporting you, until strangers start celebrating you."

If you're one of those people who finds yourself risking it all, and you happen to fail, do not let that stop you from getting out and trying it again. You truly never failed until you stop trying. There are going to be people who will try to hold you back. Don't ever let that stop you from truly doing what you love. I believe anyone can come up with a great idea and make it work, provided they are prepared, remain positive and put in the hard work. Never, ever let those who shout, "You are a failure," get an inch of room inside your head. Throughout your life, especially if you're like me and you have ups and downs, there will be people trying to live your life for you. I'm not saying, "Don't love your family," or "Give up on people who truly care about you." I've learned that as an entrepreneur who goes out taking risks and living my dreams, I've had to set up boundaries. I've had to have thick skin. This is something I share with you, because it's taken me over thirty-five years to figure that out.

In fact, this chapter also goes hand in hand with the previous one "Don't Ever Quit." It's about not allowing others to drain you, so you won't get discouraged to try or worse, quit. I keep a small square book by author Neil Somerville, called *The Answers,*[1] right next to my desk. This book has inspirational and spiritual passages throughout it. There are three that have stuck with me. I find myself constantly going back, even in today's world and re-reading these passages.

One says, "Nobody today, a prince tomorrow. Do not give up. Changes in fortune can be dramatic and swift." It's so true! Sometimes we can be so down and out, debts mounting, and have no idea of how to get out of that hole. Then, all of a sudden, one or two meetings and opportunities fall into your lap. Before you know it, within moments, you're out of the hole and you're running at full speed. It's important to understand that at any minute, your entire fortune can change dramatically and swiftly. It's also essential to never lose faith in these situations or circumstances. This is why it's crucial to hang around uplifting and positive people, not others who drain you.

The second one reads, "All comes right to him who can wait. Allow time for efforts to take effect." I can be honest and say that for the majority of my life, up until this last year, I have been a very impatient man. Sometimes it's the negative energy from others that lights a fire under you to achieve success, it has been that way with me. You have to be able to take the long view. One of the biggest things that has taught me patience is the wine business. See, it can take several years for wine to be processed. You have to harvest it, which is at least a one-year process, between making the wine and having it sit and age in a barrel. Before it is bottled and released to the consumer, it can take several years. This is a business that definitely started to teach me patience, and made me understand that it's about the long game; and most of the time, good things take time.

"Whether you think you can or you think you can't, either way you're right."

This is one of my all-time favorites quotes as I think it is very true. When you have disbelief or don't believe in yourself, you are probably not going to get where you want to go. So it doesn't matter what others think or say of you, it only matters what YOU think and believe.

Another big quote that I have hanging in my house is, "Watch your thoughts, they become your words; watch your words, they become your actions; watch your actions, they become your habits; watch your habits, they become your character; watch your character, it becomes your destiny."

This is something that really hits home for me. It is true. I've always believed that I would make it happen, and even during the darkest times of my life, I believed it and had the faith that I could. No matter what others thought about me. I think it's that little bit of faith, that little amount of "I think I can" that turns to "I know I can." It will allow you to propel yourself from any situation, at any time.

Trust me, it's an ongoing process, and one I'm still trying to perfect daily. It's important to understand this, and is a major factor when I talk to people about how I picked myself back up after failure. In fact, it's the number one question I get asked wherever I am traveling the world. It starts with ignoring negative people and your own negative thoughts, because it's very easy to get distracted and have it consume your mind. "I'm a failure. I'm a loser, look at me, I didn't make it." People pointing fingers and laughing, it happens and it's can turn into a self-defeating attitude which is at the root of most failures. I know it can seem difficult, and I know it can seem strange. But in reality, your negative thoughts are what are keeping you stagnant. It's these negative thoughts that get projected on you and that also hold people back, keeping them in misery. Remember that your thoughts are very powerful. They can keep you from seeing yourself in a way that allows you to grow and become who you're supposed to be. The Bible has a profound verse that has become a favorite of mine. Proverbs 18:21[2] says, "Death and life are in the power of the tongue." I believe this to be so true on many levels. Mind your words; mind your thoughts. They can be your biggest ally or your worst enemy.

SECTION III: THE COME BACK

XII. RELATIONSHIPS ARE EVERYTHING

There is one thing that has been a common denominator for my success – it's been my relationships. Many would consider the way I build, respect, and retain relationships as one of my strong suits. There is a reason they say, "Hang around five broke people and you will become the sixth broke person," or "Hang around five wealthy people and you will become the sixth wealthy person." We are a reflection of who we hang around and spend our time with. This is so important in life. It wasn't always this way for me, as I have shared earlier it played a role in my earlier life. Whatever bad decision I've made in the past has usually been the result of being around bad people. So much has changed since those days, and because of those lessons I have learned, I value the importance of good relationships.

I value people because I know what it's like to have people not show up for you. There are individuals who I have put so much on the line for, without getting anything in return. I have experienced some hard lessons including living through the disappointments that come from being let down by family, friends, personal relationships, and business partners. Don't let that stop you from continuing to build and foster real relationships or search for true love. My motto when it comes to relationships is, "Don't let a burnt or burned past hinder a bright future."

Let me share some stories so you can feel the magnitude of this. One of my close friends, who we will call Lucky (to protect his identity), was like an older brother to me. Though he was a big drug dealer, he was a close friend. It was one of the first relationships in my life when I was treated like family, even though I wasn't blood. He didn't have to always be there or come through, but he always showed up like a real brother is supposed to. He used to say, "Noyze, one thing at a time." He would tell me, "You got an insane hustle and speak so well, you just need to focus on bigger things." That was his way of protecting me and keeping me out of his risky and deadly business. He ended up doing some hard time, but we always kept in touch. We still catch up and check on each other to this day. It was this code and ethic instilled in me at a young age that formed the man I have become. I've learned the importance of being a man of your word. He told me something that stuck with me for a long time. "Noyze, always take care of your people, the ones truly close to you, because they are gonna take care of you." This is a key nugget that I've always remembered.

Koko was my barber back then, and this was the place where we all hung out, talked smack, and caught up with what was going on. It was on Sisson Avenue in Hartford. I remember coming off those 50 Cent shows and so many people were talking about me, especially because I was the only white guy promoting hip-hop shows and concerts. As he was getting ready to cut my hair, I was just complaining to him about how people were talking about me and saying things that were not even truthful. I'll never forget, BAM. He punches me on my chin, kind of hard and says, "Noyze, it's when they STOP talking about you that you need to worry." This was a wakeup call that would shape and toughened me up and got me ready for criticism, haters, and negative people. To be a leader, you need tough skin. It's important to keep these relationships alive.

They keep you grounded and fill you with humility. More importantly, they keep it real and will push you to do more. I've been criticized many times, and I've used that philosophy to be able to move on. "Take it on the chin" and keep moving. It takes courage to go out and make something at the risk of being ridiculed. The bishop T.D. Jakes once said, "If you don't want to make waves, be mediocre, be normal and fit in." This is so true, I'm thankful for Koko who instilled this in me at a young age; we are still friends today.

I shared about my earlier days as a concert promoter. I had a lot of successes, but I remember in the beginning there were also a lot of failures. I recall many of my first events where not many people showed up. It was very discouraging, but I kept at it. Eventually, I was able to experience big successes with a lot of A-list artists. One of the key relationships from this era was with Jason Webster. I was looking to do a college night, which was a big deal in nightclubs at the time. I asked around town who was the hottest college DJ, and it was unanimous. Everyone said that J-Dub was, hands down, the best in town.

My driver's license had been suspended for four years. Note to you guys: Don't drive on an already suspended license. I remember I had to rent cars from Hertz in a friend's name. Eventually, I hired a driver who would take me to my meetings around town. I met J-Dub at The University of Hartford. We ate at the cafeteria and agreed to do business. Thursday became our busiest night. We would go on to rock out every Thursday for over a year and become lifelong friends.

Jason and I have been friends for more than seventeen years. Since then he has become a father with two beautiful daughters and lives with his longtime girlfriend in Miami. I have taken many trips to Miami, and we always find time to hang out, reminisce, and chat about the future and being fathers. I was there not so long ago, visiting Cecconi's at the Soho Beach House, the hotel I love to stay at when I'm in Miami. We were with a few friends catching up, and he was sharing stories and said, "No matter what Chris goes through in life, he can be dead broke or filthy rich and he is still himself. He

even finds ways to get a manicure. This boy keeps his nails clean!"
We all busted out laughing. It's true – I have a pet peeve for not
having clean and manicure nails. As I got the check, I say, "For old
time's sake, let's get manicures" and off we go. After we arrived
and started to get manicures, Jason shared with me how I inspired
him, it hit different this time. He said to me, "Bro, you make
connections with ultimate ease then pull something out of each individual. You elevate them emotionally, spiritually, and even physically." Jason has been and will always be a brother to me. When I
shared that I was finally putting this book out, he was so supportive.
"Chris, you never ever gave up. You never lose enthusiasm. When
most would have jumped off a bridge, you find a way to build a new
bridge."

As I look back on these earlier relationships, which helped to
shape me, so many more friends and family members played important roles, both positive and negative that were not included in this
book. Rest assured, they are all important. I have always been real
and authentically me. I always care about people and go hard for the
ones I love. We talk about one of my best friends Ray, with whom I
share a lifetime of memories. While we were still young men and
learning our ways, Ray had gotten into some trouble and served
some time in jail. He has a big heart and was just at the wrong place
and the wrong time. I told him, "I got you when you get out," and
sure enough I did. We caught up at my club and had some laughs
and drinks to get his spirits up. Without hesitation I gave him a job
helping me. Now, it's important to give credit here to Ray, who was
a hustler and very smart. He always pulled his weight and has
played key roles in some of my biggest businesses, so it was never a
handout, it was always a help up. We all need that at times. When I
moved to Atlanta to get into real estate, I said I would be back for
him. After some convincing and help from his wife, he relocated his
family to Atlanta and helped me build my real estate company. I
remember Ray and I taking a trip back home from Atlanta and were
visiting with my mother and stepfather Terry. Ray and I took them
to dinner and were catching up. My mom said, "I can't believe that

after all these years you two are still great friends and helping each other. Ray how do you deal with Chris?" as she laughed. I mean, we all laughed because I can be a bit much. He said, "I'm just playing my position mama."

That's what made our relationship work, even as young kids barely scrapping by, the only money we had was enough to split a special number five chicken wing and fried rice. We always had each other's back, and that was just us being us. It would happen multiple times. After the big real estate crash hit and I was on the futon at his house, I again left to another city – this time Los Angeles. I promised, "I'll be back for you brother." My word to him stood the test of time and we had a great run. Unfortunately, mistakes were made, emotions ran wild in tense times, and we exchanged words. It all went wrong. At times, we often say things out of emotions or anger that we really don't mean. We had a falling out, a misunderstanding that led us to never speak again. Thirty years of brotherhood gone, it was one for the saddest moments of my life and it still affects me to this day. You see sometimes friendships, marriage, or even family can take a turn for the worse. The lesson? Learn from them. As a tribute to him, my youngest son's middle name is Ray's legal name. Many times, I tried to reach out with no luck; he was always so stubborn. Ray, if you are reading this, I love you bro. I hope someday we can put our differences aside, because life is short and precious. We went through hell for thirty years together, and I can't imagine living the rest of my life without your friendship.

Another key factor to relationships is that I choose wisely; I'm not concerned with what people think of me. I don't associate with those who judge and have constant opinions. We have all heard the quote, "Small minds discuss people and large minds discuss ideas." This is so true. I've always led from the heart, sometimes this doesn't always come across well, but it's real and truthful. It has taught me that you have to be careful about what you say. YOU OWN what you say. So many times, we say things out of anger. We say things that we don't even mean, kind of like what happened with Ray and I. These were hard lessons I had to learn and make adjustments for in order to build and foster meaningful relationships in my life.

It's important to remember where you come from. Some friends I have lost touch with, some with whom I no longer speak; some have been locked up, and some have even passed away. Relationships are work, it's important for people to know that you care for them. I say communication is essential to anything in life, whether it's a marriage, a friendship, even a business partnership.

Dolvett is another friend who has been with me through thick and thin, and we have had a tight relationship for more than fourteen years. We originally met through Justin Anthony, who is a close friend and my business partner in King of Clubs. Justin was coming over for one of my house parties and brought Dolvett with him. It was an instant bond. Over the years and through many ups and downs, we are always there for each other. Even in times I wanted to give up— because we have all been there. Dolvett will usually say something like, "Never stop being you King, consistent, detail-oriented, and a genius." I value guys like Dolvett. We have always been there for each other. Relationships like this are important.

Meeno Peluce is not only a longtime friend and like a brother to me, but he has had a vital role as the "chronicler" of the Kingsway. He is a very well-known photographer and filmmaker working with celebrities like Lady Gaga, Snoop Dogg, Lebron James, Demi Moore, and others. Meeno is unique and unapologetically himself. As a young successful actor, he was no stranger to the bright lights that fame brings; he was featured in *Voyager* and his sister played the famous Punky Brewster in the namesake hit television show. Still, none of the fame, glitz, and glory he's experienced at a young age has ever changed him. We've always had an incredibly deep connection. Over the years, Meeno and I have worked together, and he has been behind the scenes. He has shot all the campaigns for my design work, and he has done most of the imagery you have ever seen from me in press, magazines, and social media. He even shot my first wedding. And he'll shoot the next one.

I remember coming to Meeno and telling him how Rob Dyrdek and I had gotten together to create CCCXXXIII. I knew I didn't want to do it without him. We were in a creative meeting at the Soho House one afternoon before the launch of the company. The team and I were sitting around discussing the first campaign and photoshoot since we finally had the products. We began to look and see which models we would use for the campaign, and the next steps in putting the shoot together, when all of a sudden, Meeno jumps in and says, "No way. King, you are the brand! It's your energy, and your swag that's the force behind it. We are going to shoot YOU with your product kid!"

This was the first step in me actually representing the brand from a creative point of view. Our first shoot was brilliant and magical. Whenever Meeno and I work together, it's just absolute creativity, pure bliss and nothing comes close to the feeling and energy we share. This is the reason why we have been working closely together for over nine years, and why I am loyal to him.

When we were choosing cover images for this book, he was nice enough to share this with me. "King, you are a scrappy kid, bare knuckling your way through the American Dream. Underneath the luxury, behind the mask of success and opulence, you have a dream. You are wrapped up in that dream, it's still a sleeping giant, but you are ceaseless tossing and turning, you keep churning out diamonds, and you live up to your true potential. When your mother-load finally comes in, damn! That'll be a sight to see."

Another thing about relationships that I think a lot of people struggle with is this – we don't give enough credit where credit is due. I hear so many stories of people making it in life and forgetting the people who were there, or they have significant accomplishments and take all the credit. What they are not realizing is that it is those relationships that allow them to succeed.

There's this big misconception about being "self-made." This false understanding is that we've done this all by ourselves. That is not the truth. Being self-made to me is someone who, no matter the adversity, was able to pick themselves up and out of situations and strive forward.

No one does anything by themselves. If you pick anyone successful in this world, for them to have accomplished their goal, there was a loan, a friend, a family member, a mentor, an introduction or someone who gave them a shot. We all need one another. In the same way that you have gotten opportunities, you can give also give opportunities. I've been blessed to play on both sides of that equation. I've had people make life changing connections for me, and I have been the guy to make life changing connections for someone else. We always must remember and cherish those who have helped us along the way and remember those who we can lend a hand to.

When I was initially building my brand CCCXXXIII, close friends of mine, Justin Granath and Jerry Meng, were excited to help. I've known both these gentlemen for more than eight years, and we've all been there for each other countless times. On separate occasions, they told me about this respected young man in the fashion industry. They felt I would have a deep connection with him. Within days I was connected to Ugo Mozie on Whatsapp, as he happened to be in Africa at the time. Ugo is a creative executive who has worked all over the world with brands like Balmain and Chanel among others. His clientele has included Justin Bieber, Celine Dion, Travis Scott, and Beyoncé, just to name a few.

Immediately there was a connection made over text. We both exchanged comments and started following each other on social media. There was a real vibe between us. We agreed to get together when he got back in town. This was another instant bond. From the moment I sat with Ugo, I thought he was this bright, knowledgeable, positive, and humble guy.

We knew we wanted to work together. Ugo will go on to share how he admired my passion and what I was trying to build. I had Ugo join the team and work with me in overseeing celebrity outreach. Like I've shared in this chapter, relationships are everything to me. Ugo, as young as he is, understands and values relationships. It is the reason why he's been able to build such an incredible network and accomplish all that he has before turning twenty-eight. As I would go on to create collections and creatively drive the business, Ugo was there leading the way with connections and getting the product in the right hands. He is the primary reason why you see my products in the hands of celebrities around the world. We've gone off to photoshoots together in Italy, bonded, and built a true brotherhood. We are so similar but also so different. We are curators passionate about our mission and goals, while always being there for each other.

In life, you will also come across amazing people whom you bond with and have a great mutual respect for, while sharing ideas and facing challenges together. Another one of those is my great friend and business partner, Chris Harder. Chris is an entrepreneur and philanthropist whom I met at a birthday party about six years ago. While having dinner, we discovered that we had a lot of mutual friends. That night, we agreed to grab lunch soon thereafter and from that moment on, we formed a really great friendship. Chris and I are always pushing each other and strategizing on how to help each other when we can.

Chris was the very first podcast I ever did. This was something that I had turned down a hundred times over the last four years, but because I gave him my word, I would do his first. We catch up often and I enjoy spending time with him and his wife Lori. I remember even showing up for the podcast still hesitant about doing it. He said, "Most people don't get to see your heart and how much you care about people. They need to get an inside perspective about why you are so detail-oriented, obsessed, and relentless and the most unapologetic human being ever. People need to hear your story. You think bigger than everybody else. You push people bro, you need to tell your story."

I have always been the guy who just wants to make everything better. No matter what it is. I will take whatever your plans are for business, a workout, or for life and I'll stretch them and expand them. I'll give you reasons why you should be thinking bigger. It's who I am deep down, and Chris was one who returned the favor. He got behind his following and helped to introduce what I was doing to hundreds of his clients around the country. His involvement was impactful and it led to him becoming an investor in my company.

Even the relationships that aren't working will teach you things that you need to remember and pay attention to. An example of this is my relationship with my father. It never really worked out. However, while we don't speak, I also don't hold a grudge. I have been able to forgive him and have moved on with my life. Even through all this, it was instrumental in making me into a great father. I remember the first day Zachary was born. I was in the hospital with my ex-wife as she gave birth. This was such an emotional moment, as I got to hold him. While tears were rolling down my face, I realized how precious and beautiful he was. The very first thing that came to mind was how could any parent ever leave, abuse, or even disown a child? I felt the exact same way when my second son Cruz was born. The most rewarding relationship thus far in my life has been being a father to them. Words can never do justice to my feelings.

It's also important to know that not every relationship you enter in has to be about business. I have several relationships that have nothing to do with business but everything to do with a genuine friendship. There are going to be people who will be there for you with no strings attached, whether you go through hardships or not. They are the same people with whom you can share visions and ideas; they are friends who don't need anything from you, but who are willing to share a mutual passion and care for you.

Relationships are the backbone of life, whether it's a relationship with a significant other, your children, your parents, your friends, and even God. It's how you value and treat those who matter. If you don't cherish them and show up for what is important to them, I can guarantee you that they won't be showing up for you. It comes down to those people who matter the most.

The relationships I speak about in this book have been an integral part of my success. I've committed time and effort in building all of them as illustrated in this chapter and scattered throughout this book. All of them have been significant. All are key components and have contributed to my growth as a man and as an entrepreneur. Your network really is your net worth!

XIII. THE ART OF GIVING BACK

Giving back is an intensely personal thing for me, and I usually don't talk about it. I rarely even use my social media platform to discuss my charitable giving. There are several areas in life that I believe should be private. I am always donating, and I am always involved. I just don't broadcast it. When there is a natural disaster or something else unfortunate happens, I give back naturally. However, I choose to keep this private for many reasons.

A bible verse that guides me in this area is Mathew 6:1-4, "Take heed that you do not do your charitable deeds before men, to be seen by them. Otherwise you have no reward from your Father in heaven. Therefore, when you do a charitable deed, do not sound a trumpet before you as the hypocrites do in the synagogues and in the streets, that they may have glory from men. Assuredly, I say to you, they have their reward. But when you do a charitable deed, do not let your left hand know what your right hand is doing, that your charitable deed may be in secret; and your Father who sees in secret will Himself reward you openly."[1] This is something that I not only agree with but take very seriously.

I challenge you to incorporate giving into your own philosophy. My way isn't the only way, it's just my way. No matter your situation or your position in life, you can impact somebody. To take it to another level, sometimes when we give sacrificially, even if we are not yet where we want to be financially, giving out of faith is a huge step in the right direction. This can lead to a complete life change. Whether you give a little or a lot, it doesn't matter. The gesture is what will be remembered and, who knows, you may inspire someone to do the same in the future. Philanthropy is truly the gift that keeps on giving.

You need to recognize your own good fortune in life. You have heard the term, "Work hard, play hard." While this is sort of true, I would also acknowledge that you also need to give something back. Upon reaching the top, we need to help those who are less fortunate than us or those who hit a rough patch and need a hand.

Whether it's anonymously to a church or to help people in dire situations, I have given at times when it is needed. I also believe that it's important to help family and friends who are in unfortunate circumstances. There have been moments in my life when I received press or attention that I didn't want. The following stories are examples that I feel comfortable sharing.

I remember it was Christmas 2016. I was friends with a local reporter who was doing outreach for the LA County Sheriff's Department in Compton. Her mission was to help families who were caring for others in the community. Unfortunately, these families were going through some tough times. She requested that I help a specific family who was struggling to make ends meet. They didn't have a working stove. The husband would work without ever complaining, and he volunteered for those less fortunate, especially young people in the community. What touched me was that this man lacked so much, and yet he still woke up every day with a smile on his face, always giving back. The same was the case with his wife and kids; they never complained and made the best of their situation. I felt pulled to help; it weighed heavily on my heart. I rounded up some of my guys and we were able to deliver a brand-new stove right before Christmas. We even installed it so that his family would have something to cook on. Let's just say that we wanted to make sure that they had a blessed Christmas, so we threw in some other special things to make it extra special. It was such an emotional time as we were in their home talking and chatting with the children. It's these moments that make life worth living.

The reporter wanted to give some attention to this on the news. Of course, I was grateful and humbled. While I understand the importance of showcasing the noble work that charities embark on every day, I try to keep ninety-nine percent of these acts of kindness or charitable contributions between the people I am helping, myself and God. In fact, I remember the following year she reached out with new families in need. This time, I replied with a sweet text back saying, "I do want to help, but I don't want any press this time. I just want to be a blessing." This was sent with a little Santa emoji. I gave from the heart and that was enough for me.

It's also important to set boundaries and make sure you're looking to give to people who genuinely need help. Be intentional with what you do in giving back, just like you are with your life. Above all, we should all give something to pay it forward when we can. This is the basis of all real philanthropy to me.

I believe that everyone should find an organization that they are passionate about. For example, a few years ago, I was introduced to Jennifer Howell. She is the founder of The Art of Elysium, a charity that believes in building a community of artists who give back through their artistic endeavors. She told me, "We started in August 1997 with absolutely no intention of starting a charity. It was just a volunteering program at the Children's Hospital. I was able to coordinate it because I had been through their volunteer training program."

She began to tell me her powerful story, and I was deeply moved. Jennifer lost Steven, one of her close friends to Leukemia. He had been treated in a Los Angeles hospital, alongside another very sick young boy. He was alone the majority of the time while his parents had to work to pay for his treatment. Steven had told Jennifer that he wished that something more could be done for young patients who were left in the hospital by themselves. This was the call to action for her. She quoted St. Francis of Assisi who said, "In giving, we receive." She has helped more than 43,000 young people in New York and Los Angeles since 2014. This is at the heart of the programs she has created. She inspires countless other people to follow her lead.

The Art of Elysium is an incredible program. They have gone so far as to host an annual red-carpet event (which is the evening before the Golden Globes in January). Some of the past hosts have been performing artist, Marina Abramović and British fashion designer, Stella McCartney. This fundraiser raises most of the charity's revenue for the entire year. I know the kids absolutely love it. I had been so moved by The Art of Elysium's work and humbled by Jennifer's compassion that I knew I wanted to help and do more. I was on their board of directors because I believed in the amazing things that they did. I wanted to support them.

I found out that artists would constantly donate their art to the charity. After so many years, The Art of Elysium had received so many donations that I noticed they were running out of places to store it! It was all piling up in closets. – immediately a lightbulb went off in my head, and I decided to quickly put an event together. It had been a short two months since my involvement, and I was excited at the idea to host a private fundraiser in my offices in Beverly Hills. I would create an art auction. I had less than two weeks. However, the majority of my prosperous friends, who I knew I could count on were out of the country. Regardless of the challenges, I proceeded ahead anyway. There was no cost for the art since it was all donated, so one-hundred percent of the proceeds would go directly to the charity. It resulted in an amazing event, and we raised over $60,000 in less than two hours with an intimate group of friends and family. The arts have always been a source of inspiration for me. Through the most difficult points in my life, I have been able to find happiness through a song or a beautiful piece of art. This is why I love the opportunities that The Art of Elysium creates for kids. The organization gives the people they serve a chance to make their time in the hospital more peaceful, while also introducing them to a new positive outlet. They learn to access the art on their own, any time they need to find peace. It was such a blessing that I was able to help and impact them.

XIV. LET THE WISDOM IN

I have a confession to make, I'm not the smartest guy in the room.
In fact, I don't ever claim to be. If you're the smartest guy in the
room, you're probably in the wrong room. Get comfortable around
people who are smarter and better than you. If you think you know
everything, you have already lost the game. Hang up your hat. Go
home.

You need to apply the same fundamentals in business as in your
personal life. It is important to surround yourself with smart and
positive people. I've realized long ago that this is the only way to
grow. I'm always surrounded by people who are smarter or who
motivate me.

I apply these principles to everything I do; I mean everything. I
play golf. I don't want to play with people who are worse than me
(well, not a lot worse!). I want to be challenged by people who are
better players than I am. I've been able to play with a few professionals, and because they are that much better, they make me play
out of my skin. I've been able to play eighteen holes usually in the
low to mid-eighties. Now this might not be impressive to most, but
for someone who rarely gets out to play, this is great. You learn

from watching what they do, and how they do it. It accelerates your game and helps you excel. I have played with the best in everything I do, it doesn't intimidate or phase me, but it pushes me to become my best. As you get more comfortable with this philosophy, it will help you become better, and eventually, excel. This is my strong belief, and I am convinced that it will help you grow.

Even as a kid growing up, I would go to inner city playgrounds, and play basketball in some of the rougher parts of town. At first, I got my butt kicked, but I was determined to stick with it and get better. So, I kept showing up, proving I had heart. Eventually, I got better and the guys who pushed me around and from whom I caught a lot of hard elbows, started showing me some respect, and they became my friends. I got a lot better, improved both my ball handling and my shot. All this because I went out and played with the best.

It's the same with how I became hooked on fine wines. I opened my mind, and let the wisdom in. It was one of those gloriously balmy June evenings – still 65°C outside. I headed out for dinner at Cecconi's, a popular Romanesque eatery on Melrose Avenue in West Hollywood, owned by the Soho House & Co. I've been a member of the private Soho House for several years. While I'm a member of all the houses, I spend most of my time in its exclusive West Hollywood hangout, a creative haven for people in the media and arts scene in LA. Cecconi's is a popular go-to Italian restaurant for non-members and is open to the public. I parked the car and was greeted by the parking staff as I sauntered through the front door. I was decked out in a fine cashmere jacket, a neat purple and light blue checked shirt and well-ironed fawn-colored pants. The place was always filled with high energy.

"Good evening, Mr. King. So good to see you again," said the manager. "I've got your usual table."

I certainly have a soft spot for Cecconi's because it was here that I once ordered a whole truffle from the menu. I recall the waitress's eyes nearly popping out of her head as I confirmed I wanted the whole white Urbani truffle. It was this young waitress's first night working at Cecconi's. It weighed almost a pound and was massive and very expensive. A white truffle can go for $6,000 per pound. It was unorthodox for a customer to buy this at a restaurant. I mean it just wasn't normal. But this was something I would totally do, and I did. I am a truffle maniac. For those who really know me, and have spent dinners either out and about, or in the privacy of my home, you know! I devour them, and have even been called a made-up name, a Truffle-leu-pagus. Since then, I have become close friends with Michael and Marco Pietroiacovo, otherwise known as the "Truffle Brothers." Born and raised in Italy, they are now the premier supplier to restaurants like Cecconi's. The family has been in the truffle business for two generations now, and their love for truffles dates back to childhood.

Thousands of miles away, and less than thirty-six hours earlier, a specially trained beagle had identified the pungent aroma of this delicacy, before it was scraped from the undergrowth beside a beech tree in a Piedmont woodland. It was in season, boxed up and flown by air freight to the Truffle Brothers facility in Los Angeles, before making its way to Cecconi's.

My obsession with truffles is part of the story of the refined Mr. King. As I began to learn about the finer things in life: art, food, wine, fashion, and yes, truffles – an evolution, a personal one, was taking place. It is a sign of growth, and its byproduct, wisdom. One story that illustrates this well is after my initial experience with truffles. (I told you, I am an addict!) I was at Per Se, the internationally acclaimed Thomas Keller establishment in New York City, which has three Michelin stars, and serves technically classic French food. Keller is one of the few American chefs to hold three Michelin stars, so his restaurant is a culinary highlight for those who fancy themselves a foodie.

This is one of those experiences I remember like it was yesterday. I was in deep conversation with Justin Anthony, my wine partner, as the waiter came by to shave truffles over my dish. At Per Se and most high end restaurants, they shave the truffle, and weigh it before they put it on your plate, to know how much was used. Truffles are so expensive, especially white ones. So, the waiter says to me, "Mr. King please tell me when to stop." Without missing a beat, and still looking at Justin I said, "When your knuckles start to bleed." The whole table and the waiter busted out laughing. I mean of course, I was kidding, but my love for truffles goes deep, just like my love and passion for wine.

Ok, sorry, I got sidetracked with truffles. Back to Cecconi's. As I look up from the menu, I see Halle Berry, the Oscar-winning actress, who is at the table facing across from me. She's laughing and joking with a group of friends celebrating a birthday. I notice a very distinguished older man in his late sixties who is with her, and is looking for a bottle of wine. I call over the waiter and say, "Send them a bottle of King of Clubs, one of my wines. Whenever I can, I love sending a bottle for someone to try.

"And for you Mr. King?" says the waiter.

I already know Cecconi's wine list very well, and decide on a bottle of 2009 Gaja Barbaresco, one of the prestigious names in northern Italy; it's one of my favorite go-to red wines when the list at an Italian joint like this is limited. Nebbiolo is the grape variety behind the top-quality red wines of Piedmont, northwestern Italy, the most notable of which are Barolo and Barbaresco. Nebbiolo wines are distinguished by their strong tannins, high acidity, and distinctive scent – often described as "tar and roses."

I had the grilled octopus, followed by the Dover sole, while my guest Kenny Kemp, who was one of the people who has helped me write this book, ordered bruschetta and crab ravioli. I am not a big white wine drinker. Often, even with fish, I choose red wine. That is unless they have one of my favorite white wines, Chevalier-Montrachet "Les Demoiselles." This splendid wine is produced in the south of the Côte de Beaune on a very small vineyard, encompassed on less than two acres. Chevalier Montrachet "Les Demoiselles" is produced only with Chardonnay grapes, fermented and aged fifteen to eighteen months in oak barrels before bottling. This vinification highlights the unique qualities inherent in the fruit of this great vineyard. It offers a profound fragrance of toast, honey, and white fruit.

It is full-bodied and powerful, with a long finish. Made to age, this wine will develop in the bottle for fifteen to twenty years. This is why I prefer and have cases of the 1994, although I often find myself drinking the 2008, while I let the 1994 age just a little longer.

Kenny asked me a question, "How did you develop such an energy and passion for great wines?"

His question was the starting point for a deeper discussion about how we can develop our tastes in life – and how you find the essential energy to do the things you love.

I was brutally honest in answering. When I was younger, I simply didn't like wine, or at least I had an idea of what I didn't like, simply because I tasted some cheap vino that put me off. I was like ninety-nine percent of the population when it comes to wine. I was too scared to order a bottle and had little idea of what to choose. I had graduated from earlier days of fruity drinks like french connections and margaritas, and then later fell hard in love with champagne. I did not like red wine. Period.

When I moved from a little apartment in West Hollywood to a home in Beverly Hills, it was my neighbor Greg, a guy with amazing energy, who was an assiduous wine collector and who challenged me.

"Can I be honest with you about something?"

"Sure, what is it?"

"The wine you're drinking doesn't match the kind of cars, clothes, and watches you like. You're drinking two-buck chuck."

I was taken aback by his honesty, but I must say that I admire Greg. Most guys might have just said nothing, afraid that I would be offended, I wasn't. I embraced it and started laughing. You see, so often in life, people are so stuck in pride and ego that they don't allow others to really teach them something new. If I had acted that way, or had been rude, I probably would've never embarked on this journey where I found my passion for red wine. I truly enjoy it now, and it's become a major part of my life. This passion led me to owning my own namesake wine, all of which would have never happened if I wasn't open to learn, if I didn't let the wisdom in! So many times, people are easily offended, and never really get a chance to experience or learn something new. This stops us from growing. You need to understand that not everybody's going to be able to say things the way you'd like to hear, sometimes people are rude, but mean well. In fact, some of the biggest lessons of my life came with a rude, snotty type of delivery. An important lesson that I have had to discover, and I believe a lesson that most of us must learn, is that you have to be able to soak in knowledge. If you're going to rebuild your fortune again, like I did, you've got to be able to learn. You can't ever feel like you're too smart to acquire something new. This is a big lesson that has been an instrumental part of my growth and being able to reinvent myself several times over.

Greg was about to change my palate forever! "All right then, Greg, teach me." He knew his stuff, so that was a great opportunity to absorb something new.

Since we were in California, he started with American wines from Napa Valley.

"So, Greg, tell me which is the best wine from Napa?" Without stalling, he replied, "1994 Harlan Estate."

My attitude was, why not start with the best and see where this would take us? I asked Greg how we could get a bottle – and how much it would be. It was around $1,000 a bottle he said, raising his eyebrows. So right there, with Greg next to me, we went online to his trusted source and ordered a bottle. We selected overnight priority because, well, I can be impatient. Ha! We ordered it, and it would arrive the next day. I said to Greg that he should come over to my house the next evening, and that we would get some Italian food to go and crack open this bottle of wine. This was the first time I had spent more than fifty dollars on a bottle of red wine! The next day, Greg came around to my house, and we sat around the dining table. The bottle came wrapped in protective packaging, and I was extremely careful as I unearthed the glass bottle. This was indeed $1,000 a bottle. Wow! Greg popped open the cork and decanted it into a Riedel crystal decanter. We let it sit for a few minutes, then I poured two glasses. The color was outstanding, a beautiful ruby red, and even before I raised the glass to my nose, I could smell the fragrant bouquet. Its aroma was like nothing I had ever experienced in my life. I was mesmerized by the nose on this wine. When I took that first sip, it nearly knocked me on the floor. It was mind-blowing. It was spectacular; I could taste smoked herbs, cedar wood, and even a little hint of coffee and black currants. It had a massive body and balance compared to anything I had ever drank before. It was phenomenal, and I remember how long the wine just lingered on my mouth. I was hooked, and at that moment, I knew that I was never going to drink cheap wine again! Damn you Greg!

After that superb evening, I went back online and bought five more bottles. I still have a bottle of '94 in my wine collection today, and it reminds me of that evening with Greg. I was hooked and I started to gravitate towards Napa wine, learning more about the classic vintages. Greg helped me develop my taste, offering his view and suggesting appellations such as Shafer, Schrader, and Dominus. I began to develop the ability to discern the differences about what I liked and what I didn't.

I studied the basics about Napa; wine temperature, different type of grapes, and how each wine should be properly kept and stored. I admit, I was a bit vulnerable, because I didn't want to look like a fool. My education was underway, with Greg as an occasional share-a-bottle tutor. I became a bit obsessed, and desired to learn more. You know, there is nothing wrong with being vulnerable as you gain knowledge about something. Sure, I might ask a crazy question (as they say, there are no stupid questions) that a wine snob might think is stupid and naïve, but it is all part of the learning path. It was all part of the process that allowed me to be as knowledgeable as I am today. Remember, we are once beginners at something. Don't let it ever discourage you.

I had tried the best that America could produce at the time, so what about Europe? I was in the Peninsula Hotel in Beverly Hills, and I wanted to try a luxury French wine. While I consulted the sommelier in the hotel's restaurant, I selected blindly and decided to splurge a little. I asked for a $3,000 bottle of the 1983 Château Margaux, a combination of Cabernet Sauvignon and Merlot. This was more than anything I had ever spent in my life on wine. I will never forget the aroma. It stunk like horse-crap. It had an essence of mildew, dust, muck, and soil. Most people would recoil at such a body of smells. But I was turned on. To me, it was and still is like a magic potion!

I took my first sip. I never thought I could be that impressed again after the '94 Harlan, but this was something on a higher level, much higher.

It started me on a frenzy of exploration in exceptional French wines. I began to learn about Bordeaux, and my obsession began. I started buying more wine online and looking at catalogues.

'89 Petrus.

'90 Latour.

'82 Mouton.

Margaux.

Le Pin.

I couldn't stop! I had to have them and many more. I bought a wine cooler, and then I needed another one. Then another, which I put in the garage. I was hooked. I couldn't get enough. I was buying by the case and the box.

One New Year's Eve, I was visiting NYC and decided to have dinner with a buddy of mine, Jayvon. We decided on one of my favorite Italian spots in NYC, Nello's. It is owned by Nello Balan, and as it has been in business for more than thirty years. It has a European crowd feel to it. It is the go-to spot for high-priced Italian. After dinner, we headed over to the Barclays Arena in Brooklyn, where Jay-Z and Cold Play were performing. Jayvon had us ushered into the back hallway and down into the dressing area's backstage. He is Ty Ty Smith's younger brother, Jay-Z's long-time friend, and business partner. I have known Jayvon since my early Atlanta days. We always found time to catch up and share some laughs. That night I was introduced to Emory, a guy with such tremendous energy, positivity, and respect. After that evening, after I headed home back to LA, Emory and I kept in touch.

It was Grammy weekend a year later, and Emory invited me out to the House of Blues on Sunset Boulevard. Upon arrival to its quiet VIP area, I was introduced to Beyoncé, Rihanna, and Jay-Z. It was all pretty chill and friendly. I was admiring Jay-Z's watch, which was a Jaeger-LeCoultre Reverso watch, he had engraved as a memento of his Carnegie Hall concert. We chatted briefly about our preferred timepieces. I had on my Greubel Forsey, Double Tourbillon 30° with a navy crocodile strap. Then somehow, we started to talk about wine and Sassicaia, in particular, which I just started dabbling in. I mentioned I had bought a case of 1988 and 1997, and that I was in love with this Italian wine.

"Man, you got to try the '85," said Jay-Z.

Emory chimed in, "Yeah it's the best!"

The next day, on Jay-Z's recommendation, I hunted down two cases of '85 Sassicaia, which cost me nearly $50,000. It was and still is a mind-blowing wine. It continues to impress me each year.

I was tasting, comparing, and drinking about thirty-six bottles of wine a month. I was having so much fun, learning, and educating myself. There is a rarefied world of the professional wine connoisseurs who judge and write about wine. This is an admirable occupation and some writers are incredibly well informed. When you pay for your own wine though, you look at it from an entirely different perspective. Later, when we came to refine King of Clubs, my partners would say it was my experience and my taste-buds, that helped us produce such a great wine.

I was invited out to Rick De La Croix's Miami home. He was a guy with immense energy and fun to hang out with. Rick and I are both wine lovers, and one of the moments that defined our friendship, was an evening at Mr. Chow's in Miami. It was a large group of people, and Rick and I made a friendly bet. We were both given a wine list and had a $500 budget. The rules were that within that budget, we had to pick a phenomenal wine. We made this funny bet because he joked and said that anybody with money like us could just pick the most expensively rare bottle. However, if you only have $500, can you pick a fantastic bottle? We both agreed to have the waiter wrap the bottles and bring them out so we could taste each other's wine. To this day, I crack up every time I tell the story. We happened to order the exact same bottle of wine from a wine list featuring more than seven-hundred bottles! We even ordered the same all the way down to the same vintage! At that moment, we just laughed and knew we would be lifelong friends.

On October 12, 2015, we were at his house right outside of Miami. There were about six to eight people whom he had invited for dinner and drinks. I didn't realize that I was going to be part of the floor show as I walked in.

Before even settling down, Rick said, "Come on King. Tell us the wine!" urged Rick, as he brought out a large glass of glorious ruby wine.

I swirled it and smelled it. I knew. "It's too easy. I don't even need to taste it." I would know this wonderful aroma from a hundred paces. Then I sipped it.

"A Harlan," I declared.

"Get the hell out of here! Howdaya know? Yeah, you're right. So, what's the vintage?" continued Rick.

"It's a toss-up between 2009 and 2011. But knowing you, it's 2011."

"Get the hell outta here!"

He pulls the bottle from behind his back, and it's a Harlan 2011.

Let me be clear. *I'm not a master sommelier.* I do not always pick wines from regions that I don't know. But since I consume a lot, and have the experience, I have a great chance of telling you what it is by the nose and tasting it.

Once again, when you are willing to be vulnerable, and not claim you know everything, you find that vital energy to learn. Then, you can do almost anything. In this case, it was training my palate. It doesn't have to be a $1,000 bottle. It doesn't even need to be $200. For starters, you should start by smelling the wine, expecting the flavors to waft in through your mouth and nose. Then try and visualize what the taste reminds you of. Every wine has its distinctive note and, like music, you need to learn the stave. It can be done. Every time you practice, you get better and better. I recommend that you find good friends whom you admire, who either enjoy the wine with you, or teach you as Greg did. This same idea goes for any hobby, talent, or skill you want to develop. Take the time and find company to help you acquire wisdom, and if not, find your own way to make it happen.

XV. EXPERIENCE IS YOUR BEST TEACHER

In the manically busy weeks leading up to Christmas 2013, an unexpected call came from Olimpia, the VIP relations manager for Louis Vuitton's Rodeo store. I have grown close to her since becoming a regular shopper at the Beverly Hills store. She was always very friendly, but today she was bubblier than usual.

"Hi Mr. King, how would you like a front row seat at Louis Vuitton's fashion show in Paris next month?"

"How could I possibly refuse!" I replied.

She was bursting to reveal another big special surprise for me too.

"You will *ab-sol-ute-ly* adore what's being planned. But I can't say anymore," she teased.

It turned out to be a visit that deepened my understanding of the nature of premium luxury, the passion that people have for craftsmanship, and how my impulse for European-inspired elegance is lodged somewhere deep in my own DNA.

Although I was a frequent client at their Rodeo Drive store, I imagined that such a gift would have been granted to one of their top spenders; I was most certainly not it. Olimpia and her colleagues had voted me as one of their favorites. Whenever I went into the store, I was always kind and courteous to everyone, and we always enjoyed laughs together. I knew they appreciated how this made their working day more fun. I have witnessed too many spoiled, wealthy idiots, who are rude and uncivil to those who are simply trying to serve them.

A few days after Olimpia's offer, a gild-edge embossed card arrived at the house from CEO Michael Burke of Louis Vuitton. It detailed the trip and gave a clue on the upcoming Paris excursion, including a tour to Bordeaux. Some folks might not get excited about this, but the menswear show in Paris is truly unbelievable. It would also be my first fashion show in Europe.

If you are ever fortunate enough to get an invitation like this, you need to accept graciously, enjoy every minute, and learn as much as you can. I intended to soak it up.

The surprise was an invitation to fly from Paris's Orly airport to Bordeaux on a private aircraft to stay overnight at the famous Château d'Yguem. I would meet their CEO, Pierre Lurton for breakfast, and then head off to Château Cheval Blanc for a private tour and lunch. Now at this point in my life, I was in true red wine obsession form. I was a massive wine collector, and shifted gears from my earlier days with Greg collecting Napa wines, to being a full-blown Bordeaux fanatic. Cheval Blanc happens to be one of my top five favorite wines from France, so for me, an invitation to Bordeaux was an out-of-this-world opportunity.

As always, I wanted to travel in style, so each outfit was planned, matched, and properly packed. I had a trio of spacious trunks, LV of course, as I prepared three outfits for each morning and afternoon, with full evening wear, including my specially made, one-of-a-kind, Tom Ford tuxedo. It was this beautiful black and white silk jacket that today is one of my favorite patterns. You see, for me it's always about dressing up and looking your best. Every time I am in Europe, I overpack and am excited to dress up each day. I always pack spare shoes to give me plenty of options in case of wardrobe malfunctions, or if the weather changed.

My first-class flight from Los Angeles International Airport on January 15 to Charles de Gaulle Airport was with Air France, an airline who always provides impeccable service. La Première is limited to nine seats on the lower deck of the mammoth double-deck, 500-seater Boeing A380. The seats are suitably private and transform into a bed where I could fully stretch my six-foot three-inch frame. I follow the same routine when I fly. After being shown to my seat, I change into sweats, usually the spa collection from Brunello Cuccinelli, and get comfortable. This time a glass of Bollinger La Grande Année 2004 certainly put me in the mood. There were several food courses, devised by Michelin-star chef, Daniel Boulud. Starting with a crab consommé, then a main course of short ribs, green beans and asparagus, all served on Air France's seahorse design China. I had a bottle of water and a glass of 1999 Château Palmer. After dinner, I took my Nyquil Z, a sleeping tablet with an antihistamine. The ten-and-a half-hour flight in first class always passes easily. Somehow, I manage to sleep on a passenger airliner. It is something about the white noise of the engine that shuts my brain off and allows me to sleep.

It was very chilly in France when I was greeted by LV representatives as the airline's VIP attendants helped me with my baggage. I was whisked into Paris in a very familiar vehicle, a Rolls-Royce Phantom, just like the one I had at home. I was off to the Four Seasons Hotel George V, just off the Champs-Elysées. I was quickly out of the car and escorted to my private suite with an enormous balcony. I always request one, so that even during the winter months, I can enjoy a cigar. This allows me to take in the city. The Four Seasons is an opulent place with a wonderful understated elegance. This hotel will always have a place in my heart. As you would expect, their wine list is world-class. I know because I have had several private tours of their cellar.

One of the Four Seasons Hotel's greatest treasures is the George V wine cellar. To say that the entire Le Cinq team is proud of it would be an immense understatement. Its rich history has witnessed world changing events, even as far back as World War II. Designed in 1928, the very rocks that were used for its foundation were the same stones that were used to build the Arc de Triomphe.

The famous sommelier, Eric Beaumard was summoned to revive the spirit of its wine service and in 1998, was appointed Vice-President of the World in Wine Stewardship. Beaumard was passionate about his job, and made various trips to numerous vineyards in order to meet local wine experts and producers. He was the ideal man for the job. He combined his relationships, with his expert knowledge of wine, to develop and discover some of the best wines of all times. He joined forces with grape growers, while preparing for the Wine Stewardship contest in 1998. His relationship with the growers was so special that they would actually bring their personal bottles from their wine cellars so that Beaumard could present them in this legendary hotel.

After settling in, I started to unpack as I always do whenever I arrive at a hotel. I next had lunch. I summoned the wine list, and I noticed that not only did they have a plethora of French Bordeaux wines, they also had the 1986 Lafite. With its deep history, today it is still one of my favorite French wines.

The Lafite estate's vineyard was organized around the seventeenth century when it first began earning its reputation. The year 1234 is perhaps one of the oldest years, in reference to the name, with Gambaud de Lafite, the abbot of Vertheuil's Monastery. The name Lafite is of the Gascon language which means "hillock." Lafite was later found in the early eighteenth century in London's markets. The 1707 London Gazette reported that the wine was being sold at public auctions. A foreign merchant ship had been seized by British pirates. The London Gazette described the Lafite wine and its counterparts as "New French clarets." Between 1732-1733, Robert Walpole, the Prime Minister, purchased a barrel of Lafite every three months. It was only much later that France began to take an interest in Bordeaux's red wines. The wine has such a history!

Known as the "King's Wine" and "Wine Prince," Lafite was improved upon around 1716, when Marquis Nicolas Alexandre de Ségur updated its winemaking techniques. Beyond his innovations, he further enhanced the reputation of fine wines in foreign markets and the Versailles court. He became known as "The Wine Prince." Lafite's wine became "The King's Wine," with the support of a capable ambassador, the Maréchal de Richelieu.

Maréchal de Richelieu was appointed in 1755 as the Governor of Guyenne when he was consulted by a Bordeaux doctor. History tell us that he was so enamored with this new wine, Lafite, that he called it "The Fountain of Youth." When Richelieu's returned to Paris, Louis XV told him, "Maréchal, you look twenty-five years younger than you did when you left for Guyenne." Richelieu responded, "Does his Majesty not know that I have discovered the Fountain of Youth? I have found Château Lafite's wine to be a delicious, generous cordial, comparable to the ambrosia of the Gods of Olympus." After this, Lafite's wines were the center of discussion in Versailles. Madame de Pompadour had it served with her supper receptions. Further, Madame du Barry would "only drink the King's Wine." Perhaps this is why I love this it so much along with its rich history.

So, back to my story at the Four Seasons Hotel. The sommelier immediately suggested the 1982. I knew this was about to be a fun moment. You see the '82 is arguably the best vintage in French history. Truthfully, I prefer the '86 better than '82. I had several hours to kill, so I decided to order both bottles and taste them with our wine steward. I made sure they were blindly poured for him. I won't disclose his decision, and let's just say that after the amazing moment we shared, he asked if I wanted to see the cellar. I remember having walked down several stairs and flights to get into this small door opening – as you had to duck down, in order to walk into this mind-blowing medieval cave. Each little hidden pocket and shelf area had tens of thousands and possibly even over 100,000 bottles of wine. It was absolutely a slice of heaven.

Believe me, the best wines are not always on the wine list. I had discovered so many bottles not on the list that were all magical. The cellar had the most unopened and emptied bottles of '61 Petrus than anywhere in the world. The bottles of Petrus are so valuable that they keep them in the cellar; this tradition of keeping the empty bottles keep the memory of the wine alive. Let's finish the story of my entrance to the suite. Before heading down to lunch – my obsession with always looking my best, especially in Europe, meant that I had to unpack every item, ensure my trunks were empty, and all clothing properly stacked and stored. I know this kind of fastidiousness amuses those who arrive at their destination, and simply dump their bag in the room, and disappear out to the bar or the beach. I can't do that. Even when it's a more casual trip for golf in Florida or snowboarding in Aspen. I've been told that this is on the edge of full-scale OCD, and it's always good for a laugh. I don't feel calm and ready to enjoy a vacation unless I am fully unpacked, everything must have a place.

In Paris, it took me nearly two hours to properly unpack. The furniture featured delicate French antiques with drawers lined with tissue paper and tied sprigs of lavender to deter the moths. My shirts, suits, and jackets were color-coordinated, and neatly hung. My shoes were taken out of the dust bags and regimented in line on the floor of the closest, with cedar horns left in them to keep their shape and structure. I made sure all of my socks, scarves, and pochettes were put away in drawers. I took my toiletry bag and started to line up my colognes, my La Prairie moisturizer, and accessories in the bathroom. Now, I could rest and prepare to enjoy my stay! There is a deep sense of satisfaction when everything is properly hanging in spacious closets. I felt at ease and peace. I have been this way ever since I can remember.

I was then able to go out and explore Paris. It's one of my favorite cities in Europe. The elegant boulevards were created by George-Eugene Haussmann. The parks and squares, the glass-roofed tour boats on the Seine, the Eiffel Tower, and the bustling pavement cafés where I stop for my Parisian refreshments are all a part of Paris's unique architecture. My rudimentary French stretches enough to order "une bouteille d'Evian, s'il vous plait."

My schedule was maxed out and this time I would miss out on the Louvre, and another one of my favorite art galleries, the Jeu du

Paume in Place de la Concorde, with its collection of modern and post-modern art and photography. I would also miss visiting two of my favorite restaurants and chefs, Guy Savoy, who runs several Michelin star eateries, and Alain Ducasse, who I mentioned earlier.

I am usually up between five to six a.m. at the George V. I shower, dress, and walk down to enjoy an early breakfast in peace while others are still waking up. It is always the same. Scrambled eggs, wet with shaved truffles, tartines, which is a delicate baguette toasted with plenty of Normandy butter, fresh orange juice, and a bottle of Aqua Panna water. The eggs in Paris always taste so good. As someone who is passionate about the culinary arts, I'm convinced that the Parisian chefs have mastered the art of cooking eggs. While I sip a black coffee, no sugar or milk, I scan the morning paper, reading the main headlines. It makes me feel like royalty.

After breakfast, I was taken on a special visit to Louis Vuitton's workshops in central Paris where artisans have been making exquisite signature luggage for more than one-hundred and fifty years. This is Louis Vuitton's most hallowed grounds. Here, I was greeted by an elderly, aproned master craftsman who had spent nearly forty years working for the company. He was accompanied by his assistant, who had more than twenty-five years of experience, and was still awaiting his advancement to the master's position. In impeccable English, the assistant explained the five different kinds of Vuitton markings: the grey Trianon canvas, patented in 1854, the red and beige vertical-striped canvas of 1872, the beige and darker beige monochrome striped canvas of 1876, the Damier canvas of 1888, and the Monogram canvas (interlocking LVs, diamond points, starts and Kimono-inspired quatrefoil flowers) patented in 1896. I would have been satisfied spending the whole day observing these amazing people building the Louis Vuitton cases from scratch. There is such refinement and precision in this exemplary work. In today's modern world, where mass production is the norm for so many of our everyday objects, the attention to detail, lavished on every individual item, was truly awe-inspiring. It helped my understanding and formulate more of my thinking that I use now for my premium brand, CCCXXXIII. I was so hooked, I had to be dragged away from this fascinating place.

We then headed to the flagship store on Champs-Elysées. I was greeted by some of the staff from New York. I was given a tour around the store, and then got whisked away up to their VIP location on the top floor. I started buying all kinds of trunks and bags, shoes, and scarves – it just felt like shopping heaven. I remembered that it was the first time witnessing the Macassar collection. I knew I was going to be spending some money that day. They tried to offer me their usual LVHM brand of champagne, but this just wasn't going to work for me at that moment. So, I politely asked and said that what I really would love was a bottle of red wine. Now if you know anything about luxury shopping, brands simply don't allow red wine in their locations. If spilled, it would cause major damage not only to the rugs, but also to the luxury pieces or clothing. However, they looked at me with a grin, and all of a sudden, moments later, I'm being brought up a bottle of Cheval Blanc. We were having such a good time. I even remember sharing some of the wine with the staff. We celebrated the fact that I was the very first to ever crack a bottle of red wine in the VIP room and snapped a few pictures. It was a smart play, as I ended up spending quite a large sum at the store that evening. It was a magical shopping experience, and one that I will always cherish. I will remember how amazing the staff was, especially by allowing me that bottle of red wine.

The fashion show was at 2:30 p.m. in the imposing glass structure of Parc André Citroën, where Kim Jones, Louis Vuitton's men's director, was showing his latest creations for Winter 2014-2015. Most guests were wrapped appropriately against the chill in this magnificent hall; however, I was not. I was wearing a custom tuxedo tailored to perfection. I didn't want an overcoat to ruin the silk and precision of this carefully selected outfit. The theme of the show was the arid Atacama Desert in Chile. The venue was creatively transformed by a hand-painted aerial image of the desert. We learned that Kim Jones had nearly died in researching the collection when his small plane was buffeted by winds, and severe updraft from soaring ground temperatures. While traveling to Cuzco, Nazca, and Machu Picchu, he was inspired by the landscape and the ethnic cloths of the indigenous people of the Andes. He returned to Paris and his South American inspiration was apparent in the collection, giving it a wonderful sense of continuity.

I sat in the front row and was really able to get a ringside view of the detail in the longer coats, the various scarfs made out of wool and alpaca, all alongside an inspirational collection of leather satchels and hand-held baggage. Alpaca, a woven material from Chile and Peru was the collection's mainstay. He also offered a few pieces in rare vicuna, which represented top-end luxury. A particular favorite was a gray cashmere coat with a thin purple threaded line around the fringe. The finale was a marvelous piece of theater, with nearly forty men in great clothing and dark glasses stomping up the floor. The whole show blew me away with its differing style and textures. Kim Jones nailed the Andean theme, offering a glimpse of the high mountains of Chile, Peru, and Bolivia, without going over the top.

My LV hosts could not have been kinder. I had a few laughs and an interesting conversation with Michael Burke about future plans in the luxury market. Michael told me that even back to its earliest days, Louis Vuitton and his son were always looking into the future. Anything that was new and happening, the Vuitton family were mixed up in it: The Art-Deco period, new methods of distribution, new ways of showing fashion, the new luxury of the sixties. Vuitton has always been daring and curious. There was indeed a lot for me to learn from this.

After the show, we headed to the airport and off to Bordeaux. This was my first trip to the world's great wine capital. I reached the Château d'Yquem after dark, located in the undulating countryside south-east of the city. Its honey-colored stone, bathed in floodlights, still looked stunning. As our limo crunched along the driveway, I could see a wonderfully imposing building with its gleaming white shutters that captivated me, like a storybook medieval residence where the Three Musketeers might appear on horseback with their glistening blades, or damsels in distress waiting in the rounded tower with its tiny white window. It was a stronghold of another sort, however, where the world's greatest wines are cherished and stored in the vaults.

I was shown upstairs to a grand visitor's bedroom and unpacked again, trying to speed it up so as not to miss a second. Forty minutes later, I came back downstairs to a grand sitting room where the property manager offered me a glass of wine. He showed me to a comfortable seat in front of a colossal six-foot high stone fireplace with a roaring log fire. I felt the heat of my face, and it provided heat but also warmed my soul.

This château had so much vital energy and its history and character seemed to permeate the walls. It was a magical moment where I felt curiously at home, as if I had been here before in an earlier life. Somewhere, in the depths of my mind, I had a sensation that I had grown up in France and Italy in the thirteenth century, or perhaps sometime later, when I was a European king living in a castle, surrounded by lands that produced the most sough-after wines.

Before dinner, I was taken on a personal tour by the cellar master Sandrine Garbray. For a connoisseur, this was like getting a tour of the Vatican in Rome, with the Pope as your personal guide. In the bowels of this splendid château are thousands of barrels with their heady aroma of fermenting grapes. The Sauternes is a mix of mainly Sémillon and Sauvignon Blanc. The wine in the bottle racks was like liquid gold.

Of course, seeing these great treasures was a unique pleasure. It was on this tour that I learned about the secrets of the equitable climate on the Gironde estuary where the Garonne and the Dordogne rivers merge and are used to irrigate the land. I learned how the limestone in the gravelly sandy soil helps create the distinctive "terroir" which ultimately defines the taste and province of each wine. The local communes or districts of Barsac, Fargues,

Perignac, Bommes, and Sauternes are where the vines are picked over a two-month period during the late summer.

I heard more about the château's 400-year history which unfolded like an epic novel. During the Middle Ages, the estate belonged to the King of England, who was also Duke of Aquitaine. It was not until 1453, that it became French when Charles VII was crowned king. The noble family Jacques Sauvage was given feudal tenure over Yguem with the family becoming outright owners in 1711, during the reign of Louis XIV. Increasingly, the wine was admired by connoisseurs, including Thomas Jefferson. Despite France's revolutionary turmoil, it remained in the family. In 1826, the new wine cellar was built. Yquem enjoyed a long period of prosperity in the latter half of the nineteenth century, and admirers all over Europe went to great lengths to search out the wine. Great Duke Constantine, brother of the Tsar of Russia, paid 20,000 gold Francs for a barrel of Château d'Yquem. Japan meanwhile, which opened up to foreign trade during the Meiji dynasty, also discovered the pleasures of Yquem. Add this history to Sandrine's storytelling, and the result was a magical tasting.

Later that evening, I enjoyed a sumptuous dinner with the property managers and the LVMH staff, as we tasted several more vintages. I remember sampling a '51 for the first time, accompanied by melt-on-the-tongue roasted grass-fed beef from Northern France. I was surprised by its super lightness on my palate. I then was able to compare between a '90 and a 2001. I realized that I had developed a palate for differentiating the often-subtle difference in expensive wine. It was as if the various textures were hard coded into my memory bank. Somehow, I could recall the different inflections on my tongue and then each fragrance on my nose.

Over a wonderful slice of peach dessert, I learned about the more recent people who had fought to maintain the highest standard and ensure the château's legacy. Marquis Bertrand de Lur-Saluces, son of Eugène, who became an officer in the First World War trenches during what can only be described as a terrible time for France. In keeping with the family tradition, at thirty-years-old, at the end of the war, he took over managing the estate and continued in this capacity for a half-a-century. Bertrand was the guardian of the Yquem philosophy and defended the family estates, even during the recession of the 1930s. He was president of the Union des Crus Classés de la Gironde for forty years, and instrumental in determining many legal aspects of the Sauternes appellation. He did much to develop Château d'Yquem, particularly in building its international reputation, until his death in 1968. It is such an amazing place.

Later on, I was back in my room. I simply could not sleep. My head was still buzzing. It's not unusual for me to struggle to get to sleep, with my brain in overdrive going through a mental loop of all the projects I am working on or excited to complete. That night was one of those nights.

It was past midnight when I went back downstairs. It was very quiet, with a caretaker tidying the corridors. The embers in the fireplace were still red hot, and the room was still cozy. I wandered around looking at the paintings, admiring the furniture, and the calm of this château as it moved into the night. Outside it was pitchblack, the floodlights were off and there was the distant sound of an owl. I then sat back in the seat and thanked God for this opportunity.

Somehow, with the wine and the atmosphere, I was deeply tired, so I retired back upstairs. On the glass shelf in the bathroom there was an assortment of Dior Sauvage products; cologne, soap and bath supplies, another famed French name and part of the LVMH luxury portfolio. I sprayed a few drops on my body and washed my hands with the soap. I could discern the bitter essence of bergamot mixed with the soothing lavender from Provence, and it was simply amazing. I love lavender, and always find is very relaxing, this was the trick that allowed me to finally fall asleep, and within minutes of my head touching the duck-down pillow, I was able to rest for about two hours that night.

The next morning, I was greeted by M. Pierre Lurton, the

Cheval Blanc and château's president, who was appointed by Bernard Arnault in 2004. He exuded the finest Gallic charm.

"Welcome to the château, Mr. King. We are delighted you've taken time out of your schedule in California to be with us," he said shaking my hand.

"I really appreciate the invitation to your fabulous place," I replied.

"I know you visited the cellars here last night, and we have another personal tour arranged for you after breakfast. I am sorry that I have to leave town, but I will be joining you for breakfast before we head over to Cheval Blanc."

"I'm deeply honored, Monsieur Lurton."

"Call me, Pierre, please," he stated in impeccable English.

Pierre and I had an amazing breakfast discussing his history with the company. Considering his workload, Pierre was funny, very relaxed, and talked with wonderful authority. After breakfast, before I headed out to Cheval Blanc, Pierre gave me a private tour of the locked cellar where all the vintages where kept. We continued walking through this amazing arched cellar with its tinge of dampness and mildew. Its sense of order and tranquility appealed to my eye and my nature. We saw wines even from the 1800s that were an amber, almost cognac color for the age.

"What year were you born?" inquired Pierre.

"1978," I replied.

He disappeared among the racks of bottles and quickly returned with a dusty bottle that he was wiping with his handkerchief. He handed the wine to me. I pull out my iPhone to take a picture before Pierre asks one of his assistants to take it away, box it up and have it sent to Beverly Hills. It was a wonderful gift to have received, and it still sits in my cellar to this day.

I made a fifteen-minute journey by car to Cheval Blanc, on the north side of the Garonne and east of Bordeaux. I requested to make a few stops along the way to sightsee, walk around, and take this small beautiful city in. Even though it was a cold January day, I was impressed with the neatness of the vineyard, awaiting the first warmth of spring to bud for another year. The château at Cheval Blanc was a beautiful modern building, not what I expected. However, it is a state-of-the-art facility, impeccably polished and clean. Cheval Blanc wines, whether it is the 1980s or 1990s vintage, represented perfection to me.

Pierre previously had described his feelings about the wine as tactile, like silk, velvet and cashmere, a reference point for the wine that suggested its gentleness. For me, it is the pure grace and smoothness that is impossible to copy.

We sat down after the tour of Cheval Blanc and enjoyed lunch. We had a tasting with the property manager that afternoon and we opened a few bottles over lunch. "Marveilleux, tres bien," he said in wonderful French after I correctly managed to identify a vintage. He assured me that it often took many years of experience and consumption to be able to make the difference between good and great when it came to valuable wines. While this wine was the finest of its kind, I was fascinated by the heritage of the brands. This exclusive trip began to shape my ideas and attributes for my luxury brand. While I was able to savor the moment, I realized that it was a supreme attention to tiny details that enables a company with the opportunity to create something special. That was a lesson I would not forget.

After asking me what I would like, and knowing the history and rarity of the famous vintage, I made a joke.

"Perhaps we could crack open a '47."

I jested, knowing the price in a New York wine auction was around $20,000 to $25,000 a bottle.

"Perhaps not a '47, but I'm sure we can find something special."

The afternoon included an inspection of the vines. It was still chilly and slightly overcast when we stepped out, but once we walked among the rows to a vantage point above the château, the late afternoon sun, bathed the scene in a brilliant golden light. Standing there, wrapped up, looking back at the château, and seeing the rivers weaving their way toward Bordeaux and the Atlantic

Ocean was simply sublime. I felt as if I could stand in this spot for hours soaking in the history and beautiful scenery.

The French, like their neighbors the Italians, know about living the good life. I was keen to create this in the relatively new world of California. I was eternally grateful to Michael, Pierre, and all of the people at Louis Vuitton, including Olimpia and Nicole, who I know really pressed for me be on this trip. This visit helped changed my thinking. On my flight home, I wrote copious notes about everything that had touched my heart and soul. This would all be stored up for the future.

XVI. GET THE RIGHT PEOPLE IN THE
ROOM AND MAGIC WILL HAPPEN

"If you get the right people in the room, magic will happen with very little effort." This is something I have been saying for over ten years. There is no better story exemplifying this than the journey behind the creation of my own wine, King of Clubs.

I can be a bit impatient and have never believed in the old adage, "Good things come to those who wait." This is a story about being quick on our feet, acting appropriately, and letting the magic happen.

When an opportunity arises, I will always take a look. So, when my good friend from Atlanta, restaurateur Justin Anthony, called me up with a plan, I was ready to listen.

Over the years, he had been talking and plotting about opening a restaurant in California. I always loved and admired his restaurants, especially 10 Degrees. I had been telling him that he needed to get involved in LA. Between his work ethic, personality, and restaurant concept, it would be successful, and I was always down to invest and help. Finally, the call came, although it would take a fun and slight detour on to something else.

"Hey, cuz, I have an opportunity through a friend of mine to get involved in Napa. We can do a restaurant with the Mondavi family in downtown Napa."

It was a fortuitous call. Finally, my cuzzie and I could do something together. (Cuzzie is a term of endearment he always uses for a close friend, like family, and is derived from South Africa where he was born and raised.)

So, when Justin phoned me with his proposition - and knowing about the Mondavi wine dynasty – I was immediately interested. There was a snag.

"We've got to be out there tomorrow to have a look. Can you make it?" inquired Justin.

"Tomorrow? Well that's a bit short notice as I laughed ... Talk about 'Kings speed', I'm in, I'll meet you there?" I replied.

"See you then cuzzie."

That evening, Justin flew over to foggy San Francisco from Atlanta, while I hired a driver, and took my Rolls-Royce Ghost on a five-hour road trip up Highway 5 to pick him up at San Francisco International. It was pretty short notice, so I decided to work from the car all the way there until I grabbed Justin. The car helped because there was a lot of running around for us. Napa Valley is inland and sheltered from the Pacific Ocean's breezes by an unbroken range of western hills. The southern vineyards surrounding the town of Napa are the coolest, while further north, towards Calistoga the valley is warmer, and good for later-ripening Cabernet Sauvignon grapes. Over thousands of years, the Napa River and its tributaries, which have etched their way down between the Vaca and Mayacama ranges, have carried the rich mineral deposits that make the terroirs in the valley floor so fertile for grapes. For Justin and I, the extra hour heading north up Highway 29, gave us time to catch up, as we passed some of the 420 wineries, and over 700 grape-growing plots, which attract millions of visitors during the summer.

We checked into our hotel, dropped off the luggage, and decided on Masaharu Morimoto's fine Japanese restaurant in Napa, for lunch. Justin explained more about the plan. It was to buy a building with Rob Mondavi Jr., who was going to take the upper half for his offices, while a restaurant and tasting hall would be downstairs. I was perplexed. There was something I wanted to ask Justin.

"You know a ton of rich people. You are so well connected. Why did you call *me* to come and invest in this restaurant project out of all people?" Justin replied:

Because you're the only person I know who would move quickly and if you said you would come, you would actually show up. And I had to move quickly. You've always been a man of your word and didn't have time to delay and having people saying yes, but not show up. It's a time sensitive deal, plus we always talked about doing a restaurant in California.

What people often say about me is that "I will make it happen, no matter what." That's my promise. Later that evening, we reconnected with Rob Mondavi Jr. after seeing the locations all day just to catch up and discuss the building location. The three of us met at Michael Chiarello's Bottega. With another bottle of fine Italian wine polished off, we continued to explore the practicalities of creating our own restaurant project. I finally ordered a third bottle, which ended up being a French wine. Justin nearly exploded.

"King, what the hell is wrong with you. Do you not realize that we are in Napa, and we are with Rob Mondavi Jr.! Why are you ordering a French Bordeaux from the 1980s? Order from Napa cuz."

"Ha! Justin what do you want me to do. All of the Napa wines are too young to drink. The only thing that they have with some age on it while being drinkable and that I can enjoy, are the French and Italian wines." I suddenly sensed the magic around the table, and I turned to Rob and Justin and raised my freshly poured glass.

"You know Rob, why can't they make wine like your grandfather did with Opus One or even the old Napa cabs? I feel like no one makes it like those anymore."

Rob mentioned that it was possible, but that it wasn't a consumer preference right now. A lot of the wines are made to sell in bulk; thus, they are made and priced with the consumer in mind. I immediately chimed in and said, "Forget that, what if price wasn't an option and you had the ability to simply just try and make the very best."

Before Rob could respond, Justin yelled out, "Cuz, that's it, that is ... King of Clubs. It's not a champagne, it's a wine."

It was about a year previous to this evening that Justin and his lovely wife Kelly, my two sons, Dolvett, and others were in NYC for the winter holidays. We had all agreed to meet in the Big Apple to celebrate the holiday and have some excitement. I remember how much fun we had there. Honestly, we always have lots of great enjoyment together with lots of joking, storytelling, and laughter. This was a time in my life where I was consuming a lot of champagne, which was something that I always did whenever we went to a restaurant. This particular evening in NYC, we were all out celebrating life at Catch in the Meatpacking District. We were ordering tons of champagne, and Justin makes a funny joke. "Cuz I'm gonna start a champagne called King of Clubs, and just sell it to you."

We all laughed and carried on that evening. Justin's good friend at the table mentioned that it was a really catchy name and little did I know that Justin had registered the name the very next day.

Now here we are, Justin, Rob, and me, a year later sitting in Napa Valley ... And the King of Clubs wine is born. I believe that it remains a master class in achievement and a prime example of what you can muster when you have the right mindset. The result is a super-premium red wine which prompted *Forbes* Magazine to title an article, "Napa's newest cult wine?"[1]

My rationale was clear. The fine wine market has had an impressive long run with a growth rate of nearly ten percent since 1990. One of the benchmarks is Bordeaux blue chip wines. While I understood collectors and investors were looking towards Champagne and Burgundy, I could see that Bordeaux was coming back. The market for fine wine was returning in a major way.

For example, a Sotheby's auction for Château Mouton Rothschild in Hong Kong fetched $4.1m in 2014, which was double the pre-sale estimate. If the Bordeaux Index, established in 1997, was on the rise, especially in Asia, then I felt that a prestigious American vintage should also be created.

What I loved about the idea of this new business venture was that we all loved and appreciated great wine. Like fine art, fine wine is a rare commodity. I believe that a great bottle of wine triggers powerful memories that takes you back to when you first tasted that bottle.

I could tell Rob was in deep thought about this. I mean, after all, it was in his blood. His great grandfather, Robert Mondavi had created Opus One, the game-changing American wine that had the whole world rethinking California wines several decades back.

Speaking in early 2015, Gary Boom, the founder of the Bordeaux Index's managing director said:

There is no doubt the fine wine market is in a better state than it has been for many months and investor confidence is returning. With a healthy market we are expecting new trends to emerge over the coming years ... we anticipate a reversion to the classic model of consumer-led focus on coveted and valued wines that are ready or nearly ready, for the table as well as young wines with a strong story that appeals to both future consumers and investors alike.

Yes, a "strong story" —a narrative that resonates with customers was a vital key for King of Clubs.

The Wine Atlas of the World says, "Twenty percent of the value of all California's wine comes from the Napa Valley - from only four percent of its volume. Such is the reputation of the world's most glamorous, most cosseted, and most heavily capitalized wine region. Its modern history starts in 1966, with the construction of the Robert Mondavi winery."[2]

It was Robert Mondavi who created a mission-style adobe arch in Oakville right next to his cellars, transforming a rural farming community of walnut and prune orchards, into an internationally renowned monoculture of 46,000 acres of vines. With an annual production of around 25,000 cases, Opus One competes at a different level than Napa's cult wines. Did it have the pedigree? Absolutely. David Denton, sommelier at Charlie Palmer Steak and an instructor at the Capital Wine School in Washington, DC, described the Opus One 2008:

Despite Mother Nature's best efforts to defeat winemaker Michael Silacci, with frost just before flowering, below-average rainfall, and a late season heat spell, the 2008 is a beautifully balanced, Margaux-style wine. Deep ruby-purple, it gives off scents in juicy black raspberry, black cherry, currant, fragrant red-rose petals, and purple flowers. On the palate, a zippy backbone of acidity keeps the wine focused and fine, while the mocha-and-grilled meat oak character adds depth.[3]

It sells for $200 a bottle. All of this backdrop gave me a sense of clarity.

I remember when David Schwartz and I started to design the King of Clubs label. David is like a little brother to me and has been my go-to art director and graphic designer for over 10 years. He has helped bring all my crazy ideas and sketches to real life: websites, images, logos, marketing material, and almost everything you visually see around me.

When we were brainstorming, I felt this excitement come over me with the idea to pay a special tribute to those who were before us, like an artist recreating a famous painting. We added a little respect into the design taking inspiration from the famous Opus One label. If you look at the labels side by side, you can see this. King of Clubs has an emblem representing the card-deck motif with three squiggly lines representing the three founders, Justin, Rob and myself. Then the base of the design has similarities to the Opus One bottle which pays tribute to the legendary winemakers.

When we started to make the wine, what made it such a magical experience was being in the room. My philosophy is to build the team and get the experts involved. Rob Mondavi Jr. was doing his bit. I have never pretended to be a wine-making expert. There is so much I simply do not know, and so much I learned from this process. To this day, Justin and I are so thankful for what Rob taught us about the wine making process. He simply insisted we go through every step.

I was also fortunate enough to have been able to bring my own finely tuned taste buds, having sampled my share of the finest world-class crus. You will recall my first over-the-top wine experience was a 1994 Harlan Estate, a "grand cru" from Napa. "I didn't know wine could be like that, it just drew me in," I told *Forbes*.[4]

From then on, I have had countless bottles of the very best to help me with this process: 1961 Château Latour, 1982 Petrus, 1982 Mouton, 1985 and 1988 Sassicaia, 1989 Château Haut-Brion, and so many others. All this allowed me to have proper knowledge and an appreciation for fine wine to see King of Clubs in the proper context. The next morning, in Rob's hill-top home at Oakville, overlooking the gloriously verdant landscape of neatly trimmed Cabernet vines on their stakes, Justin and I made a declaration. We wanted the first vintage to be 2010. Robert nearly had heart failure.

"It ain't happening guys," he replied.

"We want to launch the wine this year," Justin chimed in.

"Guys, it ain't happening!"

"Rob, we are not leaving this house. Please make some phone calls. We want to buy juice from the very best, and we want to formulate it."

"Guys, you are asking me to not only to find a golden goose, but for it to also to lay golden eggs. It's impossible, we are too late in the game for this vintage." By the end of the day, and some frantic calls, Rob returned.

"OK guys, I don't know how the hell I made this happen. But I think I found a golden goose now. It's up to us to use to create the golden egg."

Over the next few months, we would return to Oakville for multiple tastings of wine batches selected by Rob. At times, there were up to 150 glasses spread out over Rob's dining room table and even on the floor, each with a blend of Californian grapes. Every imaginable grape was blind tasted, from Colgin, Schrader, Shafer Hillside Select, to even Screaming Eagle. We then marked what we liked and what we didn't. Hot. Cold. Fruit. Tannins. Cherries. Blackberries. Almonds. Raisins. Vanillas. Swirling and spitting.

Sniffing. Crackers and water. Rob insisted and made us go through the process. I learned a lot during this time. We really got involved. It was Justin and I's last trip up to Napa for some final sample testing. We met Rob over at his warehouse and began some more tasting. He had a rack of pipettes where he would calibrate and adjust the blend after tastings. Then he would write down different numbers, 0.035, 0.038 or 0.037. It was mind-blowing. We could hardly drink anymore. Finally, we got it down to three bottles. We loved all three. We knew it was one of them, but we couldn't even think straight, we were so tired. We were so exhausted and our brains felt fried from the back and forth. Justin and I left with the three samples and checked into the hotel. We loved all three of the selections but couldn't pick. We laughed and said let fate decide. We called over the sommelier at the hotel restaurant and asked him which one he thought tasted best. He picked it. That's what we went with. Funny enough, it was our favored pick anyways.

King of Clubs' eventual blend is eighty-six percent Cabernet Sauvignon grown on the upper eastern bench of the Oakville appellation, ten percent hillside Cabernet Sauvignon, and four percent Petite Syrah. It is then aged in one-hundred percent new French oak barrels for two years. Only 333 bottles were produced our first year. We had no idea this would later become a business selling wine at $799 a bottle, and that it would get to thousands of bottles produced a year as it still is today under the new ownership.

It was made by people who really love high-end prestigious wine. This isn't just us doing a wine, slapping a label on it and charging expensive prices. Even Rob himself was an equity partner who has put capital up. Justin Anthony was bowled over by the whole experience.

"As a restaurateur, I get to do wine tastings at least four times per month and have been doing this for eighteen years. I thought I knew a lot about wine, however, the process of making King of Clubs helped me realize how much more I still have to learn. I always knew and loved the art of winemaking, and now I also know and respect the science of it!"

The wine has made its own waves – partly because of the price point. King of Clubs is a conversation piece for sure, but also is a very honorable and exciting business. Even with my success in other industries, being part of the team behind King of Clubs has opened up a lot of doors and conversations with people who I might not have had something in common with before. Furthermore, when something is done out of pure passion and there's no financial incentives on the surface, you are likely to strike gold and magic happens! This was the very beginning of me following my passion.

With the final samples approved and our first vintage of bottles finished in Napa, Rob ended up overnighting them to Justin and I in Aspen to taste the final product. What were we doing in Aspen you might wonder? We were there for our annual family trip. I would take my mother and children; Justin and Kelly would also join us. The Little Nell was always our choice. If you have never been or experienced it, you are missing out. It is an experience I sincerely look forward to all year round. Nestled between the white snow-capped mountains, this quaint, luxurious hotel feels like home the second I walk in. After checking in, I like to relax and unwind in the main lobby with the fireplace crackling loudly, the smell of wood burning, and the somber sleeping mountains outside the grand windows. Between the hotel suites, private residences, accommodations, and luxury amenities, there is really no place like it. The Little Nell serves as "home away from home" for some of the most sophisticated and wealthy people in the world, especially during peak ski season from December to March. Some of our favorite times have been staying in our four-bedroom residence and cooking. But when we want the best meal prepared for us, there is no better place than Element 47. The Executive Sous Chef Keith Theodore never disappoints with my favorite dish: Sourdough Rigatoni with wagyu tataki, mustard greens, and shiitake. I should also mention that Element 47 has one of the best wine programs in the country and is a longtime recipient of the Wine Spectator Grand Award. Over the years, I've enjoyed the wine pairings suggested by my good friend Carlton McCoy, master sommelier and wine director. I love to catch up, share stories, share laughs, taste different wines, and explore any new wines from their glorious wine cellar of more than 24,000 bottles. Carlton has since moved on, and now is Heitz Cellar's CEO and president. We still stay in touch.

There are so many great stories, laughs, and incredible moments, year after year in Aspen, that I would need to write a whole book to do it justice.

When we returned from this trip, it was time to get to work! We ended up getting an introduction to Larry Ruvo from Southern Wine and Spirits. The phone call lasted several minutes, and we decided it would be best for Justin and I to fly out to Vegas to do a tasting. One of the things that Justin and I believed from the start, was that comparing and tasting our wine in blind taste tests against other prestigious wines that we respected and loved was important. We wanted to show and prove that our wine could sit at the same table as these iconic winemakers. After Vegas, little did web I know that Justin I would be in for a surprise. It was September 2014, and we were notified that a tasting would take place at Delmonico Steakhouse inside the Palazzo Hotel. As we walked in, Justin and I shockingly looked at each other like "holy crap." There was a private section in the back with not one, not two, but SEVEN Master Sommeliers!

OK for those that don't know, let me explain. In the world of luxury dining, the Master Sommelier is the adjutant supporting the executive chef or the proprietor, whose name and reputation draws the customers. While the maitre d' decides who dines and where they sit, the sommelier keeps the profits turning over with a shrewd selection of wines. In a leading international restaurant, it is a third of the business. In a restaurant, the craftsman is the sommelier, someone who really understands wine. For most of us, he can be a teacher.

The Court of Master Sommeliers was set up in April 1977 to promote excellence in hotel and restaurant beverage service. It's a worldwide organization with, as of this writing, 269 professionals who are at the very top of their game. It requires dedication to get into this elite body. There are only 172 in America. A Master Sommelier has to work for a diploma to show that they have attained superior knowledge of spirits and global wines. It has become a growing profession around the world. However, it requires attention to detail and a commitment by those who become Masters, that they will provide their guests with the best hospitality and finest beverages. The reward? The recipients can place the letters, MS, after this or her name. It is an extraordinary title which garners automatic respect.

Justin and I started to open up the wines that we were blindly tasting. They were a 2010 Screaming Eagle, a 2010 Dominus, and a 2010 Harlan Estate. I then look to Justin and say, "Well cuz, we are either getting an account or closing our business." Not only was it one thing to taste wine and have someone appreciate it and want to add it to their list, but it was another thing to have the masters critique our baby.

Out of respect for everyone at the table, I won't share too many details, but I will say that during the tasting and before we began, one of the Master Sommelier's raised his glass and said "Before we begin, I simply want to say that all of these wines are beautifully created, and deserve to be here at the table together."

That's all we needed to hear, what a relief. We enjoyed the meal and tasting the wines. All of them were very beautiful. With all of the successful accomplishments that we had created, Southern Wine and Spirits took us on as a client and represented the King of Clubs in Las Vegas. It was the start of our relationship and many incredible dinners and stories. We will forever be grateful for everyone involved there in Vegas and giving us a shot.

Justin and I jumped back on the jet and headed to LA. After arriving back and feeling a sense of excitement, there was still a lot of work to do. I wanted to know what the wine experts thought of the King of Clubs locally in LA.

I knew my first stop would be to see Philip Dunn, the Beverage and Wine Director at Spago in Beverly Hills. This was and still is one of my favorite places to dine in Beverly Hills. I have such a long-lasting relationship with everyone from the dishwashers, waiters, hostesses, valets, and chefs. If you have ever had dinner at this restaurant, you know exactly what I mean. This is a regular sight as I'm walking to my table because I am so close to everyone here. I love the wonderful staff: we catch up, laugh, fist pumps are given, and we always inquire about how our families are doing. When Phillip shows up, you'll catch me veering off to visit with him. He is responsible for the buying, selling, and selection of all the liquids in Wolfgang Puck's flagship eatery. He is a noted sommelier with a pedigree.

After college, Philip Dunn moved to Seattle, Washington, where he caught the wine bug. He took a class with Shayn Bjornholm, a renowned tutor and Master Sommelier in the Court of Master Sommeliers America. Through this connection, he worked for five years with Peter Canlis's iconic Northwest restaurant, as the Assistant Wine Director. He says while he loved Canlis and learned so much - including how to be "Other-Centered" to the guest's wishes - he decided it was time to move on. He met Wolfgang Puck and his managers at Spago and joined in November 2013. In 2015, Spago was nominated for James Beard's Outstanding Wine Program, won by Blackberry Farm, in Tennessee. With this pedigree, his opinion was very important for me.

He told me, "I inherited an amazing wine list from the previous wine directors. I've had that as a tool. We have around 25,000 wine bottles in our cellars with 3,500 selections. It fluctuates throughout the years with allocations, but it remains rather consistent. I have a lot of toys in my toy box, including 1982 Bordeaux in the $2,500 to $3,000 range."

Philip buys from private collectors, but only if he has a strong personal relationship with them. He is cautious about wine fraud, and how vintage wine has been stored. He wants to be sure that the wine is original and premium quality. This was why he decided to take on the King of Clubs.

In doing this book, I asked him for his thoughts. "There is something in this about dealing with you, Chris. We met in the restaurant where you are a regular. We hit it off, and now have a personal relationship. It is one reason I like buying your wine."

Philip is also a big fan of the original Mondavi wines.

"You can sign me up. If you want to give me some late 1970s to mid-1980s, Napa Mondavi Reserve Cabernet. Those wines were astounding. Even the old Opus wines were extraordinary, and I scoop them up for Spago whenever I can." To this day, Phillip and I, whenever I am dining in, share a few of these fabulous vintages.

What is his ethos, working in such as top-flight international establishment? "We are not selling wine – we are recommending it, depending on each individual's taste and their price points. We are matchmakers. We're not here to sell something you don't want. It's all about finding the best wine in whatever price range that will make you happy."

He shares that many of Spago's clientele are sophisticated globe-trotters who are, not surprisingly, well-informed about wine, and therefore understand what they are willing to buy, whether they are from Napa or Europe. So, what does he feel about King of Clubs?

"The wine is very, very balanced, and it's a style that I enjoy. It is going back to the traditional Napa wine, and getting away from that dry-extract, super Californian high-alcohol Cabernets that close your mind in so many ways. You tend to drink a lot of Bordeaux, so I know you are trying to get some balance. You are in the New World and you're going to get ripe fruit, it is just not going to happen in California. That's great, but you don't have to have it so ripe that it changes the wine."

Spago ordered twenty-four bottles of King of Clubs for its clientele. It's an expensive wine and so it should be, when you consider the quality of what's going into it. We have turned several wine connoisseurs onto the King of Clubs and it has always received a good response."

While I am grateful for the great response that we've had, we were not done yet. With the success we were having, and expanding our distribution in new states across the country, I wanted to do something else in LA. I wanted to seek out true Napa wine collectors and have them taste as well, not just the critics, but the actual men and woman who were collectors and who actually purchase.

I knew exactly who to call. I phoned up Frank Martell, a specialist in wine sales and the Director of Fine Wines at Heritage auctions in Beverly Hills. I wanted him to invite seven connoisseurs and collectors to sample the King of Clubs in a blind tasting at Spago on September 4, 2014. This was about keeping an eye (and a nose) on my prize.

It was a lunch-time event with Philip Dunn's colleague, Rina Bussell, who was on duty that day. She set up the table around the fireplace and prepared everything. There were a few truffle dishes for appetizers, and a bottle of Cristal Champagne for everyone who arrived. King of Clubs was up against three other fine wines: the 2010 Screaming Eagle, at $2,400 a bottle; the 2010 Harlot Estate, at $1,950 a bottle; and the 2010 Dominus, also around $1,000 a bottle. Each was poured into a Spiegelau decanter, with only Rina aware of which wine was in each. The first decanter was poured into the Riedel glasses where each person was able to sniff and then swill it in around. While the atmosphere was friendly, everyone took the tasting seriously, knowing that around $8,000 of wine was spread out before them.

The Dominus, a one-hundred-point wine, didn't show up well and was not taken to the next level. The Screaming Eagle, also a one-hundred-point wine, came in third. For the tasters, it was eventually down to the Harlan and King of Clubs. It was an exciting moment, with the marks at the end going in favor of King of Clubs.

"I can vouch that is was a fair contest with no coercion. The King of Clubs Cabernet came out on top against all the other wines. Chris and the guests were having a great time. It was an unanimous decision. And, of course, he was absolutely delighted that his wine was judged the best," says Rina.

King of Clubs was favored unanimously. Frank Martell who supervised the blind taste test confirmed this. For me, this was winning the most glittering prize I could think of.

We had such an amazing time with this passionate project from our first vintage 2010 with only 333 hand numbered bottles. We had picked that number because "3" and "33" were my lucky numbers, and Justin and I didn't even think it would become a business, so he agreed with that. We thought we would just sell a few bottles to friends and do something fun. Little did we know that it would be a passion that made us grow closer as friends over several years. I miss those days.

The wine label was eventually sold. We got out while it was hot. We helped secure a new wine maker, Kale Anderson, who went on to make several more vintages which are currently being sold today across select states.

SECTION IV: THE ROAD AHEAD

XVII. PASSION LEADS TO MY CALLING

I believe the way to find your calling in life is to focus intensely on your passion. Sometimes, people are lucky to find their purpose on their own, or even more so, if they can find it early in their life. It took my good friend Rob Dyrdek to bring it out of me. Before I jump into the story, let me talk about how we first met.

It was April 27, 2015, and I was just arriving at the Amanyara resort in Turks and Caicos. I was there taking a much-needed vacation with a girlfriend I had been dating for a few years after my divorce. Rob and Bryiana where there celebrating their engagement. It was such a coincidence to have seen them, considering there were only four other couples in the whole resort that week. We really didn't see anyone else.

As we passed them, we thought it was sweet to see another couple also from LA. Let's face it, most LA folks fly to Hawaii. It's rare to see anyone head all the way to the Caribbean islands for a short break. As we passed each other, there was a friendly nod, and we kept to ourselves in our villa and private beach. I knew of Rob, but never met him personally.

I enjoyed the rest of my vacation, and we never saw them again.

That vacation reminded me of my first tropical island trip when I went off to Puerto Rico, where I devoured T. Harv Eker's *Secrets of the Millionaire Mind* for the first time. While I sat with that book, I was surrounded by steaming tropical leaves drying out in the morning, the permanent aroma of fresh pineapples in the afternoon, and the gentle sea breeze in the evening. There was a similar tropical vibe at Amanyara. It is such a wonderfully secluded paradise – and we booked this amazing private villa, with our own pool and access to the turquoise sea. It was pure heaven; I remember enjoying a Hoyo de Monterrey Double Corona Cuban cigar paired with one of the best mojitos I've ever had!

Now, fast forward to July 2016, Rob reckons it was fate – as if God was magnetically pulling us together, which I completely agreed with. Rob recalls, "It was a gorgeous Sunday morning in Beverly Hills, when an image alert popped up on my cell." On his phone was a photo of my office! While I was in search of someone who would appreciate the space, he was in search for just that!

"Wow! A penthouse office. I need to see this now," he murmured to Bryiana.

Rob could see that this was a great place, and even though it started out as a lazy Sunday morning, he phoned my agent, and asked if he could see the penthouse offices immediately.

"Sure, Mr. Dyrdek. Since it's a holiday weekend, we're closed on Monday. How about we speak again on Tuesday?"

"Nope." This wasn't the answer that Rob really wanted. Like me, he can be an impatient guy when he wants something done. Rob and Bryiana decided to take a short spin in his Ferrari down to the address. He reasoned that he could at least see the front of the building to get a real picture. Before leaving, he printed the details on a laser printer. The roads were quiet as they drove over, and they parked next to a meter. Rob jumped out. Bryiana, who was pregnant, took a little longer to reach the glass front door. The door was locked, and it required a security fob to gain access to the penthouse floor. As they peered through the plate-glass door and spied the elevators, a tall man appeared. It was Barry, my handyman, who was clearing out some final items from the office. He opened the front door carrying a box.

"Hey buddy. I wonder if you can help me," Rob said waving the printout. Barry instantly recognized Rob from his hit TV shows and let them step inside.

"Well, I'll try and help. What can I do for you?"

"I'm interested in renting the penthouse. Any chance I can get a sneak peek at the space?"

"Sure, don't think that would be a problem," replied Barry.

Rob and Bryiana headed up in the elevator with Barry to the top floor. They wandered quickly along the corridor taking in the office layout. For Rob, it was love at first sight. This was where he wanted to move his business. More than that, he did not want to waste a second and lose the opportunity. He would have moved in that afternoon if it was possible.

I was just wrapping up breakfast at Soho House, when my iPhone rang, it was Barry.

"Promise me you won't get mad?"

"What did you do Barry?"

"Someone wants to take the office," he said.

"What are you doing Barry!? I thought you were just moving the last stuff out of the office, not moonlighting as a realtor," as I laughed.

"A guy wanted to see the penthouse. It's all good. I recognized him from TV," said Berry.

"I don't care if he's on TV, what's he doing in my office Barry?"

"He's now speaking to the agent on the phone. It's Rob Dyrdek."

"What on earth is he doing on a Sunday morning at my office?" Rob wasn't settling on waiting until the agent got back to him on Tuesday. From my end, we were in discussion with a potential new tenant, but nothing was yet signed and sealed. Instead of waiting, Rob took matters into his own hands, he snapped a selfie in my conference room, and got Barry to give him my cell phone number and sent me a text with no words just that picture.

There he was, the guy I knew only from *Rob & Big*, sitting at my conference table. I laughed and thought, *That's something I would do!* I called Rob and spoke to him for the first time. It was so strange. Only a few months earlier we had nodded politely as we passed each other in Turks and Caicos. Now we were on the phone, and I'm like, "Something is up." We wouldn't have run into each other at the resort if this wasn't meant to be, I always pay attention to the signs. I agreed to head down to the office, meet him in person, and give him the full details. Ten minutes later, after leaving Soho House, I pulled up to the office in my Rolls-Royce Drophead Coupe, Rob was already there in his white Ferrari.

I remember him say, "Who is this guy?" as he saw me wearing my dark blue Brioni denim jeans, blue stripe custom suede jacket, my matching blue sunglasses, with my silk slippers. *Sunday morning casual?* Not a bit of it.

From the moment I shook Rob's hand, we both felt we were not only cut from the same cloth but carved from the same block of granite. That's how we both felt. They say you only get one chance to make a first impression, and we hit it off—that feeling has only grown, as Rob has been one of the great advocates for me writing this book.

I mentioned how we passed in Turks and Caicos and he remembered, the energy between us was vibrant. Rob wanted the space to expand his business. I told him I had really enjoyed the penthouse, but it was time for it to go. However, I was looking for someone who would appreciate and love the space as much as I did. I sensed he was someone who fit that description.

Everything moved lightning fast after this. The next day was Monday, a holiday, and we met again, ironing out the details. When the agent's office opened on Tuesday, we were ready to secure the deal. I really wanted Rob to have the penthouse. I could tell by his energy and by the way he walked around, that he would enjoy it, use it, and make it into a great space. I was happy to help with all of the arrangements to get him settled in as quickly as possible.

After the deal was done, and Rob moved in, we agreed to grab dinner and learn more about each other. It was our first dinner together and I suggested Spago. We quickly would go on to have several of these dinners and gatherings. I was learning that Rob was drawn to my epicurean world of the finest food and wines in top-class eateries, and we kept going out. Little did I know this was part of him discovering something in me that led to us becoming business partners. He has never admitted it, but I think he knew exactly what he was doing by going out with me every time. It was as if he already saw something in me that I didn't even have a clue would become my calling, and my purpose. Part of what makes him a genius, is that he is able to quickly see something in someone, just by the way their eyes light up, as mine did, when I passionately talk about what I love.

I can recall our first dinner together to celebrate our friendship, and I wanted him to savor the full-on immersive "Kingsway" experience. As we arrived and settled in, I ordered the usual caviar to start. I didn't expect Rob Dyrdek, a skateboarding legend and massive success, to have never tried Black Sea caviar. Not a problem. I was happy to help. As Rob picked up the spoon to lift a tiny mound of sturgeon's eggs into his mouth, he shrugged, "I've no idea what to do here, King."

I laughed and said neither did I my first time. It was Rob's very first time trying caviar. I told him to take his blini pancake, add some egg whites, and chives on the next spoonful, which is how I enjoy them sometimes. He already loved a good steak, but I wanted to introduce to him to a mouth-watering slab of A5 Japanese Wagyu beef, one of the finest cuts of meat in the world – at $350 a pop. For those of you who are not familiar with A5, let me take a second to dive in here. Wagyu beef comes from cattle that are bred just for the purpose of creating the best flavor possible. The cattle live a sedentary life, eat frequently, and are bred up to thirty months to create more of an evenly distributed, marbling effect in the beef. The result is a high-quality beef with unsurpassed taste. The A5 is referencing the score from Japan's Meat Grading Association that provides a score from one to five based on marbling, firmness, color, and quality. An A through C score is based on the ratio of meat to weight of cow's carcass. I even read that the National Livestock Breeding Center maintains the records of the cattle, tracing back their ancestry and history and can actually trace a steak from a restaurant back to its origins. Now that is an impressive history and details. Most Wagyu beef is either A4 or A5, according to its superior standards. I later became friends with Hisato Hamada of Wagyumafia who taught me so much about this incredible delicacy.

The story continues. As we are sitting at the table in Spago, Philip Dunn, the sommelier with whom I have a great relationship, comes to the table.

"Let's finish with the 1971 Gaja I brought, but let's start with something from the '80s French of course. How about the 1986 DeCru?" I said after I introduced Rob. "Excellent choice!" said Philip approvingly.

On his return, he surprised us with an '82 that he was holding for a special occasion. This was a pure treat, and what an introduction for Rob. I could tell he was really enjoying the evening. Now, Rob hadn't had a '82 Decru before or a Bordeaux wine from that year, in fact most of the world has never tried it. The '82 is a very special vintage in French history. For Bordeaux wines, 1982 is a historic year for a myriad of reasons. It was the first true vintage of the modern age, ushering in a new style. It was a long time coming. Not since 1961, twenty-one years earlier, had wines of this consistent level of quality had been produced. This wine is also the vintage famous for launching the career of Robert Parker, the world's most successful wine critic. Parker's non-stop, exuberant praise of this vintage, earned him the respect of a new generation of wine lovers, which has continued for more than four decades.

The electric energy at our table was sizzling. High-voltage conversation sparked between both of us. We were two guys sharing our stories, and it got more intense as we gorged ourselves on wine, caviar, and A5. My natural instinct was, *How can I help this guy who I really like*?

He was intrigued to find out more about what I did. We'd

already talked about our backstories, all about my upbringing in Connecticut, my life in Atlanta, and my move to Los Angeles. He told me about his move from Ohio to make it big in California. He spoke about his MTV reality shows, *Rob & Big* and *Fantasy Factory*.

"In hindsight, I was thinking about how much I learned, about his way of thinking, and his deep passion when he would talk about caviar, wines, or watches. He was just this very passionate guy, animated, and engaging; I must say, it was captivating," recalled Rob later. "We were talking about his bespoke suits, his crocodile custom shoes, and I'm thinking, 'This guy is all about the details.'"

This is where I think Rob began to consider the potential of having me as a business partner. But we had a long, long way to go. For now, it was about enjoying each other's company and laughing a lot. As we left Spago, still laughing and joking, we agreed to get together soon. There were many dinners and I even remember him taking me to the screening of his friend Tony Robbins new movie *I Am Not Your Guru* where I was introduced to him for the first time. We began to hang out even more, learning and pushing each other, and always laughing! It's was like I grew up with him in my neighborhood. We didn't need to say anything, but we knew we were going to do a deal. At this stage, we had no idea what it would be.

A few months later, on August 4, 2016, we were back together again in the penthouse. It was strange being in my old office as a guest. Rob had already hired builders to pull down one of my office walls in order to make a much larger conference room. He was creating his own unique space, reflecting his sense of purpose. The Dyrdek Machine is a one-of-a-kind venture studio, which creates and invests in companies using the Machine Method. The Machine Method is a process Rob developed for systematically building sustainable and successful businesses.

Rob wasn't a graduate from a big-ticket business school or a dropout from an Ivy League school, but he had accumulated knowledge and a toolkit that was a roadmap to success. As we would keep talking and sharing stories, we realized how much of the same trial and tribulations we have both gone through.

I admired how smart and thoughtful this guy was. He was far from the skateboard TV personality people perceived him to be. This was someone who really dug deep to master the specifics about business and execution. One of his favorite lines was "You must create a Tactical Financial Road Map."

"Live in the Energy" declared a sign display across the raw concrete on the wall, while the brands he had created, Pig Out Chips, Black Feather Whiskey, and Momentous Supplements, were displayed on a nearby table.

As I walked in the office, I explained to him that the previous night I had a weird dream. In the dream, I was coming in for a meeting like today. I got off the elevator, and we met for several hours. When I got back in the elevator instead of going down to my car, I went up another level. He looks at me with a smile but doesn't chime in yet. I say, "I know it's crazy, 'another level,' I mean, what's higher than the penthouse?"

"I know you thought about helping me, King," said Rob. "But the way I see it, is that I want to help YOU!"

I had clearly got this all wrong. Rob helping me? Wait a minute. This was a 180-degree role reversal for me. I was normally the one who stuck my neck out and took the risks. For the first time in my business life, this was a role reversal. Yet there was momentum, and Rob sensed this energy. After all these years, it was a case of meeting him at the right place and at the right time.

Rob asked me to write down all my companies on the white board and explain what I was doing with each business. Rob and I had spent enough time getting to know each other over the past month. So, he was pretty familiar with most of what I was doing.

"It was his hustle and diehard work ethic that stuck with me," said Rob, as he erased the board I had just drawn on, explaining to me that I needed to think differently. That the way he saw it, I needed to follow my passion.

Rob explained his business rationale to me. He laid out the

truth about Rob Dyrdek, the pro-skateboarder personality who promoted DC Shoes, Monster Energy Drinks, and Alien workshop. He talked about starting his foundation, and how he appeared on multiple television shows. He was a natural-born presenter and was at home in front of the camera. He was featured as a cartoon and even put out a movie. He told me this was all the "through line" from skateboarding. Rob explained how he built his business along the lines of this skateboarding interest and personality. It was his mini universe of brands and media. He explained how he was able to sell across the entire platform to his passionate and loyal fan base. Skateboarding was at the center of the entire ecosystem. Here was the catch. He explained, that in his early forties it had all changed because he realized that his true passion was creating companies, and so, he was building a new ecosystem around business.

"I'm not well informed about the luxury space, but you need to do exactly what I did," he advised. "You have the personality and the energy, the understanding, and knowledge. If you can apply this in the luxury space, you can create the same thing that I've done with media and television," as he was drawing all this on the white board.

"We should really do something," said Rob.

It was about creating a brand, a brand with me, and that he felt I should become the brand. He said that charismatic founders add so much value. Rob explained his business rationale to me. He had created his venture studio to build and invest in companies with people just like me and this was an incredible opportunity for us to build something special together.

There was this immense jolt for me, it was almost like "How come I never thought of this?" It sounded and felt so right. I was uncomfortable about being the face of the brand, as I was always the guy behind the scenes. Rob encouraged me. He said that I should focus on the creation of a new business platform where I would become the face of premium luxury. I would be able to develop and design a range of products that I felt were worthy of the highest standards of luxury. For Rob, it was all about capturing the kind of detail and craftsmanship that most took for granted.

"This is what you need to do – for you King. No one else. Instead of doing things for other people, let's do it for you. It has all the makings of things you are supremely passionate about. You dive into that detail. Describe form and function, while focusing on the product's craftsmanship, then you explain why it is so special."

This was the brilliant truth. Here was a new friend showing me a path for the future, and he was even lighting the way.

"So, you're not here to help me. I'm here to help you," he concluded. I couldn't stop laughing and smiling. I was nervous, scared, and had mixed feelings. He had another meeting, and I had to get going. We agreed to revisit this in a few days and agreed to meet back at his office.

As I arrived home that evening, I couldn't get our meeting out of my head. It had me really thinking about my entire life. I mean, on one hand it sounded amazing, getting to do what I love to do, kind of like the wine business but only it would be full time. Building a real luxury business on all my ideas and thoughts. It was exactly what I had ever wanted, but I never knew how to do it. Did I, or was I so focused on following opportunities, business deals, and working so hard, that I never took the time to stand back and really think, "What do you want Chris?" I was so busy with all the companies I was involved in, that I never really looked at myself as a business. That instead of investing in someone else's talent and doing all the hard work to build them up, I could, in fact, be the talent, with my work ethic, dedication, and do or die mentality. I was fired up. I went into my wine cellar and grabbed a 1989 Mouton. I pulled out the Ah-So and opened the bottle, poured myself a glass and headed into my home office.

I started to jot down all the companies I had, the problems, the upside and the downside. I realized in a moment of clarity that while I enjoyed what I did, my real passion was in fact being involved in the businesses that I enjoyed personally. It was almost like a basketball player who loves the sport so much and finally gets to go to the NBA. This was my chance. Was it my calling? Was it finding my purpose? Although I would love to tell you that it hit me in a clear moment, that this was my purpose or my calling in life, it wasn't until halfway into building this business with Rob, that it hit me the hardest.

Now I knew that this is what I wanted to do. It was unreal that I would be in charge of building a business with everything I loved and enjoyed and was passionate about. There was such excitement in me. But the crystal-clear moment that changed my life forever was when I knew I was doing exactly what I was supposed to do all along. I had found my calling and my purpose, which was fueled by my passion. This was all just a few weeks before our company would launch.

I had just finished filming some videos with Meeno and cutting up the last intricate details before getting ready to launch on March 3. Meeno had just left, and I was sitting at my desk once again, when I felt the overwhelming presence of God, and it hit me hard! You see, I've always had such a very over-the-top sense of perfectionism, bordering an OCD. I literally find myself always noticing the most minute details. It has been like this my whole life, and sometimes it can be overwhelming. I have no doubt that this is a gift from God, but at times, I've also felt like it was somewhat my curse. Over the years, I found myself thinking that maybe I should learn to not be such a perfectionist, learn to let go, and make life move at its own pace. Instead, what I realized, in that moment of clarity, was that this "curse" was now my gift, which I finally get to utilize. It was the same overly detailed mind that allowed my partners and I to build such an incredible wine business, prior to finally finding my passion, my purpose, and now my calling.

XVIII. FIND THE RIGHT PARTNER:
ENERGY IS EVERYTHING

It is essential for me to live and work with people who feed off of my kind of energy. Energy is everything! I believe that your attitude dictates ninety percent of your life. An old poster of mine reads, "Life is 90% attitude and 10% what happens to us." There's another saying I like. It states, "Attitude can make or break a church, a home, a friendship, a relationship, a marriage and a business." I couldn't agree more.

I strongly recommend you find people who share the same views on attitude, communication, and energy. Seek and find those who share the same vibe with you. I've been really fortunate at many stages in my journey, I've gelled with people who have helped me stay positive. I have had lasting friendships with various types of individuals from around the world who have all given me their wonderful injections of positive mental energy. More recently, this energy has come from Rob Dyrdek. I have finally found someone who, when we get together, is comfortable discussing a universe of ideas. It's not forced, it flows.

There's a synergy that allows us to bounce thoughts and ideas back and forth. We are both trying to help each other get to the next level. There is always BIG energy around us. For anyone that has been in the room with us, it's contagious. Just ask Brian Atlas. He is the President of Dyrdek Machine and is often with us in our meetings. Brian who has become a friend, has been involved with Rob's businesses for more than a decade. Brian shares, "When Rob pairs up with someone on his creative wave length like Chris, it's magical. I have witnessed their energy together; it's something to experience." Brian or "Prezzy," as I call him, has played a major role in Rob's companies, especially the one Rob and I are building. We goof around, crack jokes, get hyper, we have even jumped around outside with excitement about an idea or a discovery.

I was on my way back to meet with Rob, after taking the time to process all we had discussed during our last meeting. I was arriving back to my former penthouse – I occupied it for more than three years before Rob took it over. I would regularly gather the Cruzach, Inc. team in the conference room for a working lunch there. It was a trendy Beverly Hills penthouse office with views over West LA towards the hazy Hollywood Hills.

Originally when I saw the place several years earlier, it was a shell with blown-out windows. For me, Beverly Hills became the ideal place to live and work, evoking the glamour of the film industry which epitomized the American Dream, and anyone who was brave enough and worked hard enough could succeed here. I was one of the first people to move into this building. I took over the penthouse and oversaw every detail of the construction: every tile, every marble, every light fixture, even every sink was hand-picked by me. I was given the freedom to design the place and it took ten months to complete. There was a wraparound deck around the entire penthouse with superb 360° views. I created a spacious deck area where we had artificial turf to give it a grassy feel, and I put white sofas outside with six-foot palms trees in large pots around them. I also had orange sofas around the other offices. We even set up a blue ping-pong table and an outdoor gas grill for barbecues. I wanted to create the best working environment I could. Along the gable-end conference wall were hefty planks of refurbished and reclaimed wood that featured a flat screen TV, perfectly centered on that wall. On the inner partition wall hung the artwork from my friend Retna, along with works by Basquiat, Ed Ruscha, and others. The stressed-concrete flooring has a lacquered gloss of polish, while the ceiling was left bare, with exposed aluminum hardware of the heating and air conditioning. There was usually a lot of laughter and plenty of joking. There was a shared affection and ambition in our wall-to-ceiling, glass-fronted workspace.

A typical lunch would consist of two large cardboard boxes packed with glistening morsels of sushi and neatly cut rolls with pieces of salmon, crab, tuna, and halibut wrapped in seaweed and rice, the authentic Japanese hamachi and iwashi. Though they were all delicately tucked into the cartons, they would soon be dispensed around on individual plates. This was not unusual for us to order sushi from our favorite local go-to Sugarfish. Through the glass, there was a kitchen with its color coordinated white-front cabinets and stainless steel appliances, Nespresso coffee machine, and the full-length fridges filled with ice-cold drinks to keep this team hydrated. Most of the executive team members had individual offices on the penthouse floor, with sliding glass doors leading out onto the penthouse deck. They deserved this setting. I could not have built many of my businesses without my team. They know who they are, and I have always appreciated them and thanked them from the bottom of my heart.

I was immensely proud of this place. We moved into this office in 2013 and had three brilliant years there, but I was about to begin a new business path. My focus was changing. I had a wonderful home in Beverly Hills. I'd been able to create a comfortable home office, and I wanted to spend more time there. I was at a different place in my life and work-life balance was important. I wanted to be at home, around the children, and have a clear, stress-free place that helped my creative instincts to flow.

I got off the elevator, and Rob came around the corner excited, smiling, and full of energy as he always was. He was in his typical office attire a black T-shirt, multi-colored Nike sneakers, and a gold Rolex. We jumped back into the conference room, and he immediately said, "So how you feel? What do you think? We doing this?" I was excited, but still didn't know exactly what we were going to do, or how to do it. There was still a little fear about me being the front man for this new brand.

I said, "Rob, I'm excited and I want to do this, but I don't know."

At this point Rob gets up, full of excitement and says, "Chris, this is your calling, and you need to do this, in fact I'm going to be your partner, I'll even write the first check, I'm serious." He was serious. It was the confirmation that he was going to be my partner, and that I was going to do this. It is what I always wanted and dreamed about, but was too afraid to do. There he was, pushing me, and believing in me so much, that he wrote a one-million dollar check to prove it.

I remember being in shock, this had never happened before in my life. For the first time I had someone believe in me more than I did myself. He believed not only in my ability to get the job done, but in my creative ability to create and build something out of my true passion.

We started marking out possible products and ideas on the whiteboard. The energy and the passion were in overdrive. It was magic, and I had not experienced anything like this in a long time. I always say, "Get the right people in the room, and magic will happen." This was one of those moments. We agreed to start and come up with ideas and names for the company and commit to another meeting within a few days.

That evening I went home, and I started moving around companies and holdings and making the room and clarity to finally focus on myself. For once, I was going to be the face of a brand, and it was exciting. What am I going to call it? Rob and I knew from the beginning that it would be a much bigger brand down the road, but we had to have a starting point. We needed to pick something. I knew that ultimately being in the fashion industry was what I wanted, but we wanted to approach it differently. We knew that the accessory market was a big part of thriving businesses in the luxury space. That was our starting point, but we didn't have a name yet.

I was getting a manicure at my local spot. I started to think back on how many bottles we had produced with King of Clubs, knowing it was my favorite number. I grabbed my iPhone, pulled up safari, and googled "333." There it appeared; CCCXXXIII. It was faith, I loved it! It was European chic. I knew that I would source our raw materials and manufacture our products in Europe. I envisioned true European craftsmanship; it was the perfect name. I texted Rob right away, "I think I got it bro, CCCXXXIII! My favorite lucky number 333." His response was a bunch of fire emojis, and a quick text back saying, "I love it." Finally, we had a name.

I showed up at his office the next day. We considered a bunch of products, talked through the rationale. We spent hours immersed in preparing concepts. By this time, it was February 22, 2017. There was so much thought and preparation going into this. We agreed on the name, and this was what we were going to do. It was clear, we were excited! Then, all of a sudden, we raised our heads.

"Look, man. A sign," I pointed.

It was an enormous semi-circular rainbow in its full glory over the Hollywood hills. It wasn't even raining outside. With the bright sun rays coming through some of the scattered clouds, it was like a sign from God!

"It's a sign all right," replied Rob with great laughter, as he had Hurricane take a photo of this moment.

Over the next few months, we had regular sessions trying to figure out exactly what we were going to build. I would take Rob to more fine dining, and we would congregate in the penthouse over black coffee, dry erasers, and whiteboards. There were still many things to work out.

Rob explained in detail more about his own experiences and business philosophy, suggesting that I might look at this business in that way too. I concluded that I had been juggling too many businesses for too long. With too people pulling at me and several of the enterprises failing, it was a distraction. I had to declutter. While a few of the businesses were highly successful, precious energy and time was being spent on having to deal with things that I wasn't passionate about. This was the moment I dove in full steam ahead!

XIX. MY ITALIAN LOVE STORY

It all started with a phone call. I was in my home in Beverly Hills. It was an early winter morning, and I had just made myself a cup of coffee. My office is a large room filled with memorabilia that I have acquired throughout my life. Featured prominently is my giant black marble desk about eight feet long and four feet wide; it has all my Lalique desk accessories on it. As I entered the office and closed the double doors behind me, I started the fireplace. I loved to light it in the morning before working and taking calls. It was typical for me to be making calls to the east coast around 4:30 a.m. I can remember when my sons were a little younger and they would wake up, come in the office, and enjoy the warmth of the fireplace while pretending to be daddy doing business, talking on the phone and shuffling papers – all along, laughing and trying to sound like me. It was so cute.

I threw my headset on to find Djordje Stefanovic's contact number and dialed him up. As I was attempting to build this new luxury company, I knew I needed someone who understood what I was trying to do and someone who had deep connections in Europe, especially Italy.

Years ago, in September of 2015, I had met Djordje at a mutual friend's house in Atlanta. We had a big dinner gathering, and I found myself sitting next to him. He was in a perfect fitting suit and tie; I immediately respected him for his choice of attire. After all, not many men wear a full suit and tie to a casual dinner at someone's house. His tailored dark blue suit paired with his custom shirt, perfectly knotted tie, and large dark frames was impeccable. Of course, anyone with this kind of effortless style would be the one I would have the most in common with. As fate would have it, we would have much more in common than we knew. We had many laughs, shared some stories, and exchanged contact information. He was a highly ranked executive at Zegna, the Italian clothing conglomerate, and suggested we get together the next time he was in LA. Some time passed and we ended up getting together at my house in Beverly Hills during his visit. I remember that evening very well – I had grabbed three bottles from my cellar, all 1988 vintages: Château Margaux, Château Lafite Rothschild, and Sassicaia. They were all to die for, not to mention that the 1988 Sassicaia is my favorite vintage.

While enjoying the wine and grilling some steaks, we were getting to know each other better, and that was the start of an incredible bond. We even shared a Cuban cigar to finish the night. We had stayed in touch, but years had passed, and so, here I was, making a phone call to Djordje in my home office.

"Hey, Djordje, how are you? I miss hearing your voice. How's life?"

He replied, "All is well. Same here."

I started to tell him about my crazy idea of creating a luxury company. I truly hoped that he might be able to point me in the right direction and give me some insight about who I could hire or bring on to help me in Italy. After speaking for several minutes, he said, "You know Chris, I might be able to help you. I have just retired from Zegna and could take some time to help you do this. After all, if anyone is going to pull this off, it's your crazy self."

We shared a mutual laugh and began the process. Djordje came on as a consultant to help me find the right people and factories in Italy to work with. He was instrumental in helping me identify the right partners. He not only lived there and spoke the language but was deeply connected in ways that others were not. He subsequently flew to Italy the following week, on his own, to schedule meetings. Just like that, he returned, and had secured all that we needed. I was shocked, but at the same time, not surprised. You see, Djordje is a great man, a man of his word, calm, respectful, and very intuitive. He is the type of man who fosters incredible relationships, and one of the kindest guys I know. In fact, there are many things that I picked up on our journey together, things he has taught me about life, like fatherhood and being a gentleman. In fact, I don't believe that he suspected that he did any of these things.

Off to Italy we went ... We took several trips back and forth, spending weeks at a time, month after month. We went from factory to factory and meeting to meeting. It was the food, the language, the people, the architecture, and the smell, that I fell in love with, but this next trip was going to be different. It was the end of September 2017. We had arrived to handle business and production on the twenty-sixth, and were planning to leave that weekend, however a very important meeting was scheduled on Monday that we couldn't miss. Djordje had the perfect idea, "Why don't we leave our Milan hotel on Friday, and I will show you where I used to live in Tuscany. We can stay down there and see some things, not only will we save money – but you can see a side of Italy you have not seen yet. Little did I know, my life was going to be drastically changed forever.

We took the three hour drive down to a place called Tombolo Talasso Resort. This magical place is surrounded by pine trees and is steps away from an inspiring and beautiful beach. The view was a few hundred feet away from the magnificent medieval town of Castagneto Carducci. We checked into the hotel and got right to sleep. Djordje had a few surprises planned the next day.

After waking up and having a quick breakfast, we got onto the road. We pulled into Tenuta Argentiera Bolgheri in Podere Pianali, not far from the hotel. I was blown away by the property. We were greeted by a longtime friend of Djordje, CEO Federico Zileri. Not only was he the CEO of this incredible winery, but he was also the Bolgheri Consortium President, and the owner and heir to the family business, Castello di Bolgheri (which I will get into a little later in this chapter).

We walked this property and went up the hill towards the vineyards, the view was breathtaking. The lush green hills, valleys, and the Tyrrhenian Sea's pristine water in the near distance was so close you could smell the saltwater. On this clear day, you could almost make out the Tuscan Archipelago, which is a chain of islands between the Ligurian Sea and Tyrrhenian Sea, west of Tuscany. The tour lasted for hours. I soaked up every detail and was so thankful for Djordje and Federico. I found myself absorbed in all this knowledge. That day was one of those days that I will never forget – my soul was fed from their generational knowledge of wisdom. I also found great joy in learning from older, wiser men who have made their way in life. There was this undeniable feeling that I was exactly where I was meant to be, and just as I looked up while walking, there it was. A giant stake in the vineyard marked "33." They used these stakes to mark each part of the vineyard. In general, 33 and 3's, are always this guiding force, like the area marker for a sense of purpose and direction throughout my life.

I could feel my spirit soar in a very humbled and fulfilling way. Djordje noticed it as well, after all, the name of my company at this time was CCCXXXIII, which is roman numerals for 333. Snapping a picture for me, he smirked, knowing that this was an omen. After the vineyard tour and seeing all the facilities, we walked back down this path to taste some of the wine. It was this long trail, which must have been at least a mile, if not longer. It had these perfectly tall trees, their branches reaching high towards the heavens, and wide toward the horizon on both sides of the road that came together. They acted like a covering and protection for the trail, keeping the hot summer sun away. Even before asking, as my curiosity wandered, Federico chimed in. He said these trees were planted by the owner many, many years ago. His daughter would ride her horse up and down this trail. He wanted her to be able to ride in the summer months without the heat disturbing her, so he planted these trees to protect his daughter from the sun. I mean, come on … the love of a father! I could just feel the energy and love in this magical place.

We arrived and sampled some amazing wine. We enjoyed several tastings, and I remember my favorite being the 2011 Lavinia Maria. It was so good that I ended up buying a few bottles to take home with me. We were then going to follow Federico to the small town of Bolgheri, and have lunch at Enoteca Tognoni, right in the small town's center. It was right next door to Cantina Castello di Bolgheri where we would later visit to see Federico's family wines.

As we sat down and ordered food and a bottle of wine, I had the wild boar pappardelle pasta. It was so good and paired with lots laughter and storytelling. We chatted about everything. We then ordered a bottle of Federico's wine, and started to taste it. I am not really sure, nor do I remember how the conversation started, but we ended up buying a bottle of 2013 Sassicaia, and a bottle of his wine in the same exact vintage to compare the wines. I remember having this back-and-forth conversation with him about how the wines had similar attributes, while being very different. I am far from a sommelier or a winemaker, but something in me led me to be bold and declare that I felt there were things that were characteristically amazing about his wine, but if changed could be better. I grabbed a piece of paper on the table and jotted down what I believed his current blend to be. I then suggested that if he tried this blend, he might come up with a phenomenal blend. I mentioned how, years ago, I created a wine with Robert Mondavi Jr. in Napa and helped create the blend. I shared that my interest to do it again was constantly on my mind.

As he looked at the piece of paper, he looked up at me, then over across at Djordje, and started speaking in Italian in a loud voice. He then got up from the table and went off to use the restroom. Djordje sat there with his typical grin and smile. He always gives me this look when taking a few extra minutes to ponder his thoughts before speaking ... He crossed his leg, picked up his espresso, and right as he's about to sip it, he says, "Only Chris King!" followed by a chuckle.

In a moment of feeling like I made a mistake or insulted somebody, he said that Federico was very impressed that an American knows so much about Italian wine. I was relieved that my boldness hadn't offended him. Quickly I grabbed the check so we could follow him out to see his winery.

We went next door to Cantina Castello di Bolgheri. We arrived at the entrance to see how the family wine is stored and aged in barrels. At that time, Djordje had excused himself to use the restroom. Federico mentioned that he would escort him, because it was far.

Little did I know that this would be a defining moment in my life, while being left alone for just a few minutes. I looked up on the wall, there was this giant painting of a beautiful family tree. Instead of having all these leaves on the tree, they were replaced by small circles, with the first name of each family member in this generational ancestral tree. Out of nowhere, I started to burst into tears while looking at this tree and all these names. I noticed that Federico's name was in the middle of the tree. Suddenly, I felt this overwhelming sadness that I had never experienced. In this moment, I felt that I had never had these deeply connected blood lines and ties with a deep generational family, with grandparents and extended family who carried on these glorious traditions, and ensuring that each tradition is handed down heir to heir. Here, generations upon generations, have continued to build on their history and businesses to create generational wealth. It left me really emotional. Why couldn't I have this? With all I wanted to accomplish and do in life ... Out of nowhere, I felt the presence of God come into this room. He put his hand on my back. I heard this soft voice say to me, "No son, that's you at the bottom." Immediately the tears went away and at that moment, I knew that I was going to be the one to build the family tree and that I would be the one to establish and create generational traditions and a legacy. This is why I have been so focused on my brand, knowing exactly what I want to build. This was also the defining moment when it became very clear on the type of woman I would eventually want. I knew I needed to find a woman who could stand next to me at the bottom of that tree. A woman who wouldn't think short-term, but who wanted to stand by my side and build something together that would last for generations to come.

It was a moment that will forever shape the course of my life. The guys came back, and we went down to tour this beautiful place where all the wine was being aged. I had the opportunity to learn a little bit more about the winery. We then ended up heading back after saying our goodbyes and gratefully thanked Federico for his time, his wisdom, and the opportunity to taste and see both of these incredible wineries.

Djordje and I checked back into the hotel and ended up changing into some shorts and a T-shirt. We grabbed a few Cuban cigars and headed out to the beach. It was about 6:00 p.m. and the view was breathtaking. After a walk on the beach with our cigars, we chatted and watched the sunset. Heading back to the hotel, we showered, got changed, and walked over to a nearby local restaurant, La Tana del Pirata. It was chilly that night. The patio was closed, and the inside was packed.

It was really hot inside. If you know me, I hate being hot –especially if I'm dressed up and we are going to enjoy wine. Djordje asked the waiter in Italian if we could sit outside in the cold evening, where literally no one else was sitting. He looked at me like I was a little crazy and said, "Sicuro," and we were escorted outside and seated.

This is a time when I would carry around a special handmade leather red book with my initials stamped in gold. I would take off the labels from the wines I would buy, stick them into a book, and take notes about them. I would note what I ate, who was with me, and everyone would sign it. This was something I learned to do when I was in NYC, staying at the Baccarat hotel. My dear friend,

Matthieu Yamoum, the wine director at the Baccarat would do this upon special occasions with his favorite guests and taught me this.

Our waiter arrived; I believe he was also the owner. He pushed out a big tray full of freshly caught seafood. We selected some fish and ordered Spaghetti Esagerati (which is clams and prawns) along with a veal Milanese. I remember how amazing and fresh this food was. If you've never dined in a small local Italian restaurant, you should put it on your bucket list. Words can't describe it. Gazing at the wine list, the prices were insanely cheap. I recall that evening we had a 2010 Masseto, which is one of my favorite big and bold Merlot blends in Toscana. Djordje grabs the book and scribbles in, "As we would say in Italy: 'Finale col botto,' what a meal and what a WINE!"

After dinner, we had our usual espresso. I saw this look in Djordje's eyes, when he discovered that they had Cassatina Dai Dai, which is like an ice cream sandwich here in the states. He used to enjoy them as a kid growing up in Italy. He ordered one to go and, on the way out, I grabbed a few candies to bring back home for my sons. As we walked back to the hotel, Djordje had something amazing planned for tomorrow. While we were walking, the only thing he said to me with a grin was, "Sassicaia."

How could I sleep? I was so excited. This was by far one of my favorite and probably one of the most consumed Italian wines ever. I was getting to visit this winery, this enchanted place that is so difficult to get into, let alone reserve a private tasting. It was difficult to fall asleep, but eventually I dozed off. The next morning, after having breakfast at around 11:00 a.m., we then made our way to this world-famous winery. You have to understand that this Italian wine is one of my very favorites! The 1985 vintage is arguably the best Italian vintage in wine history. While I do agree that the 1985 vintage is impressive, I personally prefer the 1988 vintage. The 1988 vintage was also the great Italian oenologist, Giacomo Tachi's favorite wine, which he pronounced better than the 1985.

Sassicaia comes from the Tuscan terroir of Mario Incisa della

Rocchetta, who created his first vintage in 1968 planting cuttings of Cabernet vines from Château Lafite in Bordeaux. It has such a rich and powerful history. I couldn't help thinking about the centuries of cultivation that brought me to this space in time, and the love and attention that were poured into each bottle. The Tuscan coastal area of Maremma was not thought conducive to producing quality wines and for many years the Sassicaia was a local secret known to friends and family, while Mario concentrated on raising thoroughbred race-horses. The area created a legend in 1978, when it beat thirty-four selected Cabernets from around the world in a tasting sponsored by *Decanter* magazine in London. Since Mario Incisa's death in 1983, his son Nicolo has been running the vineyard, and production has increased while keeping the dignity of the estate. All this history! All this passion! So, you can imagine the way I felt when we arrived at this place.

Off the main road, Località San Guido, we turned onto a back road, which most people are unaware of. It led to a large gate where with a quick buzz and an exchange of a few Italian words, we were let in. As we drove up and stepped out onto this breathtaking prop-erty, I could feel the energy in the air. We were greeted and brought into the building. I instantly noticed the vast wine rooms with barrels on top of barrels of wine being aged in temperature-controlled rooms, visible through giant glass windows. They were aging the 2016 vintages, and I was there in the flesh to see it, even being allowed in to walk and put my hands on the barrels. As we came around a corner, there were three bottles in a museum-quality glass presentation, showcasing some of the very first vintage bottles. There were three bottles side by side in this particular case: 1945, 1958, and 1967. These were very different from the wine labels on the bottles that we see and know today, it was some of the first label designs. We sat down and were greeted by a woman who was our host for the tasting. Instantly we dove right into sampling the wines along with some cheeses. Djordje looked away, smiled, and looked back at me.

I sensed someone approaching, I looked up, and to my surprise, it was Priscilla Incisa della Rochetta, a member of the family which owns Tenuta San Guido Sassicaia. She is known to most as the Princess of Sassicaia. She was so humble, kind, and polite. We chatted for several minutes and ended up capturing this moment with a picture in the front grounds of the estate. She was known not to take many pictures so this was an honor and a surprise! Words can never thank Djordje enough for this special weekend. We conversed for a few more minutes, thanked them for their time, and headed out back toward Milan.

On our way, we visited two key cities. The first was Lucca, an ancient city that is known throughout Italy for the medieval walls that still encircle it. You see the entire city is isolated from the rest of the world with giant walls that must be over ten feet high. Originally discovered in around 180 BC, this Roman city was an important meeting place for notables such as Julius Caesar and Crassus. We walked around town for about an hour, before having lunch at Buca di Sant'Antonio. The Italian Porcini mushrooms arrived at the table; it was intense. Aside from truffles being my favorite, these mushrooms have bursts of intense, rich, and earthy flavors that are simply unreal. The world's very best porcini, as with truffles, come from Italy. We finished lunch and went back to the car and headed to Portofino! This incredible city was the last stop on our way back to Milan.

Portofino is southeast of Genoa City, a fishing village on the picturesque Italian Riviera coastline. Its pastel-colored houses, high-end boutiques, and seafood restaurants fringe its piazzetta. Its small cobbled square overlooks the harbor, which is lined with vessels, big and small. Castello Brown is a fortress and museum from the sixteenth century not far from the piazzetta. Castello Brown's art exhibitions and breathtaking panoramic perspectives are surreal.

As we parked the car and walked down to the harbor, we grabbed a bite to eat at Ristorante I Gemelli. Djordje explained that this is the city where pesto originated from. Naturally being a pesto fan, I tried the recommended entrée. As we dined and chatted, I stared out at these amazing harbor views, with the smell of the sea and gentle breeze in our face. I can see why this place is often considered to be one of the most charming seaside villages in the world. As we made our way back to the car, passing famous boutiques, we walked into Mingo, a men and women's shoe designer that makes one of the best lightweight and comfortable slip on shoes for the hot summer months. I couldn't resist and purchased a pair, a keepsake to take away from this beautiful city.

We arrived back to Milan and checked back into the famous Bulgari Hotel, my home away from home here. "Buona sera Mr. King," as we arrived back at the hotel. The staff, managers, and everyone are always so nice and so accommodating. Besides this particular trip, I've stayed at this hotel so many times, and I have many fond memories: From late evenings at the bar with the managers and staff laughing and sharing stories, to the funny Instagram moments (like the times when they allowed me to mix a drink behind the bar), or when I enjoyed a cigar in the lounge during a business meeting.

The creation of this exclusive luxury hotel in Milan was born out of an obsessive desire to provide luxury while sparing no expense: from the 4,000 square foot garden in central Milan, to the spa, and the optional Maserati pick up service. The rooms give a respite from the chaos that exists outside the walls of the eighteenth century structure. The warm interior lighting and décor give you the feeling that you are in your own home. I appreciate the little details like the personalized business cards they provide with the hotel address. The hotel was created to be a jewel among Milanese travel destinations. The staff is so attentive that every need is met with effortless warmth, which is not an easy thing to do, even among the most reputable hotels around the world. Here, I feel like I'm staying at a close friend or family member's home, where I can come and go as I please and really "just be."

In my opinion, it is all about the experiences, the energy, and the feelings that you have when you visit a place. It's also the fuel that leads to my creative thinking and the visions I have when I'm there. Some of my best designs and concepts have come from evenings alone in a hotel, sketching or drawing, or writing down ideas. Some of the best captured photographs in Milan were during a previous trip when my dear friend and photographer Meeno was with me. I was tired and drained from constant fifteen-hour workdays. It was our last evening there. Meeno suggested that I put on a tuxedo and go with him to shoot some images. I looked at him like he was crazy; it was almost 1:30 in the morning. We had an early flight, and I was exhausted. But in true King spirit, I went upstairs, took a cold shower, threw on a tuxedo, hand tied my bowtie, and completed the look with my velvet slippers. I met Meeno in the cigar lounge, and we enjoyed a cigar and drink to get ourselves in the mood. Before we could finish, we took the cigar and glass of port and walked around the streets of Italy. As we were walking and laughing in the moonlit streets of Milan, Meeno was snapping photograph after photograph. I'm so grateful that he pushed me to do so. Some of my favorite images ever captured by him, and the images I prefer to use for press materials are from that evening. No crew, no lighting rig, no assistants, just us and our energetic brotherly bond. In fact, the very image on the front cover of this book was captured by Meeno that evening. Out of all the years of working together, we both agree that this evening in Milan was one for the record books.

Djordje and I checked into each of our rooms after the long drive from Portofino and prepared for the next morning's meeting over by Lake Como. Now, let me start by telling you that I have been to Lake Como a dozen times. I have dear friends that run the city, own restaurants, boats, villas, and I am so blessed by their gratitude and open arms every time I visit. Lake Como is literally a slice of heaven in the middle of Italy. Como will forever be embedded in my heart and is one of the key components in this Italian love story. It is where I learned about patience and calmness. A magical energy comes off of the lake, like a gust of wind flowing over it, and enters into your lungs and into your soul, the realization at Como is that you are in a place unlike anywhere else in the world. Some of my dearest friends live in Como: Carlo, who I speak with weekly and is instrumental in helping me make key introductions, like Mario Boselli, president of the Italian Fashion Chamber; Alberto, my driver when in Italy; and Luca, who always enjoys taking me out on his Riva cigar boat for a cruise on the lake when I visit. These are just a few of my close friends from this dreamy city.

After our meeting, we went and had an espresso at the famous Villa d'Este. This is one of Italy's most iconic properties on Lake Como. It is surrounded by impeccable gardens that span over twenty-five acres. Two historic mansions provide accommodations dating from the sixteenth century. The décor in each room is unique with exquisite and luxurious furnishings, silk drapes, fine linen sheets, and oil paintings. The hotel spares no detail. The distinctive Jasmine smell is by far my favorite part; I love the smell of this white petite flower. There is an overgrowth of these around the entire property overlooking the lake. I always sit outside in the morning while having breakfast. I am so content with my eyes closed, just smelling these Jasmine shrubs and feeling the breeze off the lake while the sun hits your face. It is just such a distinctive smell and feeling that you have to experience at least once in your life. This is one of the many reasons why wealthy patrons, celebrities, and a loyal clientele keep returning time and time again. Let's not forget to mention the unmatched level of service and the "floating" pool that afford the most breathtaking views of Lake Como. I've stayed here on the property several times and each time is just as memorable as the next. This Renaissance Hotel always makes me feel like a king from a distant past. There is so much in this region to love; for example, I also love to visit Hotel Royal Victoria in Verona, it has also been the location for some of our photo shoots.

The following day Djordje and I headed back to NYC. I fell in love with this wonderful country, from my initial trip with Djordje to a succession of visits to cities like Florence, Capri, and Roma. Each city and each visit left me with a new perspective. I have had so many priceless experiences: from visits to the outskirts of Parma, where I have discovered ancient churches and to the time when I had a private tour of the "Last Supper," the famous painting by

Leonardo Da Vinci. Each time I walk the cobblestone streets, whether day or night, winter or summer, I slowly and naturally fall in love with Italy yet again. So many places, attractions and restaurants like Giacomo Bistrot, Anitca Osteria Cavallini and Dal Bolognese are just some of the few where Djordje and I love to go. I can't name them all, perhaps I need to make a coffee table book! I have met life-long friends in this magical country, like Cristiano Belloli the owner of La Bullona in Milan, which is among many other venues and clubs he owns. Him and his longtime girlfriend Kate are like an extended family to me. Another great bond I have made is with Francessco Bassi (of Bassi Partners) who leads one of Italy's leading construction management company. He works between Milan and New York City, and we always catch up at Antica Trattoria della Pesa, a small restaurant with antique furniture and the best ossobuco, the famous classic Milanese dish. I will forever love and adore the country, the people, my friends, and everyone who has touched my heart, created memories, and birthed the profound realizations that are with me. They will last a lifetime. Thank you Italy!

XX. TELL YOUR TRUTH

I get goose bumps whenever I watch the Academy-Award-winning movie *8 Mile* staring Eminem. There is a scene in the film that tugs at my heart. He is up against one of his opponents and gets to go first in this final battle. Here is this skinny, fair skinned, little "B-Rabbit" in a tank top in front of a hostile and amped up crowd. He is the minority, and what he does next against his opponent is not expected. He gets to go first and grabs the mic and denigrates himself in front of the crowd.

"I know everything he is about to say against me. I am white. I am a bum. I do live in a trailer with my mom," he cleverly admits as he raps with power and intent. Eminem takes every punch. Then when he's done, he hands the mic to the opponent. There is nothing left for him to say. It is the turning point of the movie, and it still gets me pumped up every time I re-watch it.

We live in a modern world that is swirling with constant negativity. Especially today with the rise of social media and keyboard warriors who just fly off at anything without an understanding of the real world. People want to see you torn down and pushed into the gutter. You may realize that other people – who don't even know you or your circumstances, may speak badly about you. They have no idea about the real you, or what you have been through. Yet they criticize, judge, and talk behind your back. I have learned that in today's world we are no longer in charge of our reputation. One can make up stories, reviews and lies anywhere online. We are however in charge of our character which ultimately is our true self.

You can take that negative power away from others by owning your mistakes and flaws. By taking control, you allow yourself to grow stronger, and you learn to become better. You can make the decision to control your mind and not let the negative stuff impact you. I have used this as fuel my whole life. Your weaknesses will now be your strengths. I've been broke. I've lived in my car. I've had the barrel of a gun shoved in my face. I've seen people shot and stabbed. I've had my father walk out. I've failed at business. I've been through a divorce. I've made countless mistakes. I've been jumped, and beaten up by fifteen guys outside a gym, and so on. I've been through so much. So, what are you going to do to me? What's the worst that's going to happen? This doesn't scare me. I am not afraid of going back to where I started, I am afraid of not trying! I am not saying you have to go through what I went through, but there is a unique power that lies within you enabling you to confront even the smallest insecurities or flaws.

Let me tell you about something I have discovered about a nation that has taken a calculated risk in order to not succumb to poverty. I had this realization on a flight. I had a few extra days off after a business trip to Paris, and instead of flying straight home to LA, I decided to head to Dubai. It is an amazing city that has fascinated me as a super-modern metropolitan magically springing from the desert in the last twenty years. I was flying first-class on Emirates Airlines, a wonderfully luxurious experience, enjoying it from the comfort of my private suite, complete with its own entrance and flat screen television. You must experience this airline at least once in your lifetime. I was blown away. Even for someone like me, who appreciates luxury and has flown in private jets count-less times, I was impressed with this airline. I got comfortable, ready to enjoy a movie, when one of the air stewards came around.

"Would you like to take a shower before you land?"

"Excuse me? Did you say a shower?"

"Yes, sir. We have a full spa facility."

A shower on a plane at 35,000 feet, flying at 500 miles per hour, so that I can refresh myself before we land! Amazing. I thought it couldn't get any better as I flicked through the entertainment. My beautifully presented cuisine arrived next.

"Would you like some wine with your meal?" I said, of course I would love some wine. "What do you have?" I inquired.

She handed me the wine menu. I couldn't help but notice that they were offering a 1988 Château Palmer by the glass. I look at the stewardess and asked, "I can have a glass of this Château Palmer for no additional charge?"

"Yes sir, that's correct."

"I can have unlimited glasses of this wine, at no extra charge?"

"Yes sir, and I believe we have a few bottles left."

"So … Can I get the whole bottle and one glass, please?" I smiled somewhat knowingly. She smiled back and brought me a bottle of 1988 Château Palmer. I enjoyed this as I started to watch an inflight documentary called *Red Obsession*.[1] It was made by an Australian filmmaker and narrated by Russell Crowe. If you are a wine connoisseur or someone looking to learn about wine, this is an outstanding documentary. Like the moment in *8 Mile*, the film had a section that resonated with me intensely. It explained how the booming economies in Asia have developed a taste for French wines, and how this region had become a leading market for purchasing high-quality Bordeaux wines.

They interviewed Ch'ng Poh Tiong, a wine journalist and publisher who begins to explain that the Chinese have made most of their money in the last thirty years. The documentary goes on to explain that China was able to build fully operational skyscrapers at a fraction of the time it took to do so in the United States. This was the same with vital infrastructure such as roads, railways, bridges, and dams. China has become an economic miracle, taking calculated risks to build its powerhouse economy and allow a new breed of entrepreneurs to emerge, such as Jack Ma of Alibaba and Zhang Ruimin, the founder of electrical white-goods giant, Haier Group. This is all at a time when the United States has been losing millions of jobs, and where trade unions have failed to read the playbook.

Here is the point I'd like to make. Ch'ng Poh Tiong went on to explain that he believes the reason why the Chinese economy has grown so quickly is simple. He said, "If they've lived through the Cultural Revolution, this means they've gone to hell and come back. So, when the Chinese do things as is so obvious now to the modern world in a business venture, or any venture, for that matter, the Chinese have no fear. Because they say 'Well, how worse off can we be? We can just start from zero again.'" It wouldn't bother them at all. This is why China is so dynamic. People shoot for the stars. In the documentary, they showed a shocking time-lapse video of a thirty-stories skyscraper being built in China in just fifteen days. I mean that's only 360 hours!

This resonated with me. Why would you not risk it all, and work your butt off? That's what I have done time and time and again and probably will my whole life. I remember his words clearly, "Well, how worse off can we be? We can just start from zero again." He is speaking the truth. I gained a lot of knowledge from that documentary. It's good to take risks to build a life. I can see that the Chinese have been doing it! However, you need to make sure that it is a sound calculation, and that the risk has a real upside for you and your future.

For me, there have been moments and opportunities to tell my truth. As I was building my real estate business in Atlanta, we started to do exceptionally well. I then hit a large hole in the road when it came to loans. The business was growing rapidly with investors in both Houston and Chicago, but we had a major issue in

Atlanta. As we got deeper into real estate business, things started to move. However, we had trouble getting the loans approved, in order to sell the properties fast enough to keep up with the demand. We had critical issues that could have sunken our business.

One afternoon, I was being fitted for a new suit in Atlanta. I was standing in front of the mirror and chatting with Mark.

"How's business these days? Still going well?" he inquired as he measured the sleeve and marked it with a fine line of chalk.

Now, in this moment I could have said what most people do, "Business is great." I could have covered my truth with small talk and shrugged it off. Instead I decided to be honest and transparent.

"Well, we've hit a big roadblock with finance, so we're having some major troubles until we get around this," I replied.

Now, in times like this, most people might not say much, they might judge, and some may even laugh at your misfortune, and gossip. However, Mark continued:

"You should meet another of my customers," he suggested. "I can introduce you to Sam. A major player and the VP at SunTrust bank here in Atlanta and a very nice man."

"Sure. I would love to meet him," I replied, shocked that he would be so kind as to want to help.

While I was in the dressing room, putting my pants back on and adjusting my necktie, Mark took the opportunity to call Sam's office. Surprisingly, he was put right through.

"Hi Sam, it's Mark here."

"Hi, what can I do for you?"

"I'd like you to meet another of my customers. Mr. King, who is in real estate. He's a smart young guy who could use some help, and perhaps you two can do business."

"Sure thing. Get him to call me."

Later that week, a lunch was arranged with Sam. I needed to reverse engineer our situation. I focused on trying to align myself with a bank that would have a strong financial position and could service my customers quickly and efficiently. We needed the bank to understand what we were doing, so we could move quickly, and not get stuck with our properties for too long. Anybody can buy a house, fix it up, stick a "for sale" sign on it, and then wait till somebody comes by. But each month you wait to sell, there are $8,000 to $12,000 in payments, due per house, and it soon adds up. If you weren't careful by the fourth month, the hard money lender was saying, "Your loan is due – I want my money back."

This was becoming a risk for us as we were building, renovating, and constructing a lot of places. Now we had a bank that would get these properties closed for our clients and close them fast! It was a lifesaver, all because I was truthful in a time when I needed help.

There are so many times in your life when you will have the opportunity to speak the truth even when it's not comfortable, even when it might not give you the outcome you want. This was the case when it came to writing this book and why it was shelved so many times. I didn't want to relive my past, put my business out there, and talk about the ups and downs, embarrassing moments, or times of ridicule. Recently, there was another moment of truthfulness that completely changed the direction of my current business and led to putting this book out.

It was October of 2019, and I ran into a friend, Amos Pizzey, while having lunch at Cecconi's. It had been years since we spoke last. We quickly agreed to catch up at Soho House later in the week. Amos was someone I had met when I first came out to LA. He was building a company called Talent House. He had come from a rough upbringing in the UK and went on to being signed by a major record label as a young artist. Subsequently, he learned the ropes on his way to becoming an advertising executive for Saatchi & Saatchi. He was rough around the edges but wore his heart on his sleeve. He also carried himself like a gentleman and shared the same code I did.

During our lunch he told me about his new company, 3rdsoul and I shared about what I was doing. We connected about being a gentleman, and I shared my views and what I was trying to do. He shared how much he respected what I was building and agreed with me how important the modern gentleman is and needed. He then began to educate me on the "Knight's Vow." I was fascinated as I had never heard this before. He began to tell me that the Gentleman's code in the western world originated from the tenth century Knight's Vow, "Be brave in the face of your enemies, always tell the truth, protect the helpless, do good and be upstanding so that God may love you." Over many generations, this chivalry code was passed down from titled knights. The term "Sir" is originally derived from the officers across all the armed forces, ultimately influencing all of modern society. For a long time, referring to someone as a "Gentleman" was the highest compliment you could pay a man. This would lead to a big revelation.

Little did I know that another old friend would unexpectedly confirm the alignment of all that I was learning about this Knight's Vow. His name is Reverend Ardell Daniels, who I met through my good friends, Bill and Jennifer who were close with him. He happened to have a layover in LA years back. Bill brought him over to the house. As soon as I met him, I recognized that there was something very different about him. He was calm, humble, and I could tell that he was anointed by God. We prayed a lot that day and built an incredible bond that has lasted several years. We are constantly catching up, discussing ideas and ways to impact and help others.

An interesting thing happened as I was having a casual catch-up conversation with Ardell. It would unlock a piece of information that would connect Ardell and I further and bring clarity on what was to come. On December 26, 2019 I was sharing with him about the new direction that I was taking with the Christopher King brand. I shared how important Kingsway and the Art of the Gentleman is and that I recently had discovered the Knight's Vow from Amos, as I shared earlier. He began to laugh and said, "Chris, brother, you know I am Bishop Daniels, a titled knight of the Jerusalem Grand Prelate, of the Order of Knights Hospitallers of the Sovereign Order of Saint John of Knights of Malta's Ecumenical Order." This entire time, I was learning about the history and rich knight's codes, and Ardell not only happened to be one, but was the ordain priest for them! It was all lining up.

Months later, around December 2019, Amos and I were catching up for dinner. We started to chat and order dinner, Amos bluntly asked, "What's wrong?" I was having great success with my brand CCCXXXIII and coming off a great month. Major celebrities like Beyoncé, Justin Bieber, and All-Star athletes were publicly carrying my bags. But something was missing, I needed to take it to the next level. I felt our company name was too complicated to understand and pronounce, especially in the US.

Amos chimed in, "King, you're just more than a wealthy white guy, flying around the world, holding nice bags. You're putting ethos around what you are doing. I think that a large part of your audience are younger people who are going through this journey themselves. They don't know that you are like them, that you are not this generational wealthy guy, you are self-made." He went on, "This, to me, is what makes your brand interesting. You had a very tough early life, your beginnings in hip-hop and street culture and the fact that your father left early on, all contributed to you having to step up to provide for your family. Tell these stories, share with the world the real you, King."

He made me really think about it, what came out of this meeting was that he was telling me to stop hiding my truth and to stop hiding my story. It was one of the same reasons I shelved this book years ago. I worked so hard to build a better life and climb out of the gutter, that I never wanted to look back or share those stories. I worked diligently to establish myself as a gentleman and become self-educated. I taught myself how to properly dress and act with manners and chivalry – I never wanted anyone to know about my rough upbringing. In a sense, I had taught myself the Knight's Vow without even knowing it. I felt that if others knew the truth, then they would not want to work with me. My truth was that I didn't go to some fancy school to learn how to be a designer or go to design school or any fashion institution. I built a luxury company, received major *press attention,* even landing in the French edition of *Forbes*[2] Magazine for my collaboration with Aston Martin. All of this without a formal education. But yet, I didn't want people to know where I was from. What I learned in this moment of clarity is that my truth is what sets me apart. It was all lining up again.

Amos and I were recently building out the narrative for our new direction. In a meeting at my house, he was fired up pacing and telling me my truth. He started to say, "King, you are an extension of the self-made man in America. Not just bringing high-end luxury goods to the marketplace, but educating people as to why." He went on to say, "You demonstrate what loyalty means. You're very empathetic and have deep religious faith, which I greatly respect greatly. You're motivated by the idea of doing something for the greater good. You represent chivalry and a return to excellence, the Art of the Gentleman, and this is why we need to tell your story."

Immediately, it started to hit us. Amos wanted to help me tell my story. He had this idea to dive deep into my truth and share the story with the world. It led us to finally creating what would be the beginning of my brand's identity. Together sitting down in the conference room with Rob, Brian, and myself, we got back to the original conversation that Rob had inspired in this exact room. We talked about how the brand was me. My past, my flaws, and my mistakes, all had led to this moment. It was time to expand my brand and grow it from CCCXXXIII, to Christopher King Inc.

Amos jumped up super excited, and chimes in, "I think that Chris has (which is tremendous) what I call, 'energy of manifestation.' When you're around Chris, he creates and shares that energy, and it is infectious and leads you to believe more in yourself. That's really the mark of a founder for, really, anything. You know what I mean? Founders are good at inspiring those around them to have the same vision.

"I believe what Chris is really doing is inspiring people to think about their behavior. And that's a very powerful take right now. I believe in what he stands for. I think he's good for the world. His positive energy has motivated me to do better, to go harder." Since these meetings, Amos has gone on to great success and is now the head of music for TEG.

It was my moment of clarity; it was telling my truth; it was my time to share my story to inspire others.

XXI. THE ART OF THE GENTLEMAN, "KINGSWAY"

I have always been fascinated with The Renaissance and Ancient Roman era, centuries ago. Many of the very things I have instinctually picked up have had their genesis to that period. The Art of the Gentleman, or as I like to call it "Kingsway," is the very foundation of my businesses, my brands, and my life. This concept of a return to chivalry is at the heart and soul of "Kingsway." I believe in this simple truth, "Manners make society." I truly believe, now more than ever, that it's important for us to return to chivalry.

Why is all this important to me? It just makes me wonder. Whatever happened to the art of being a gentleman? Where did we lose all of this? Have the morals, chivalry, and actions that garnered the respectable term "Gentleman" been thrown out with our suits and replaced with athleisure and streetwear? With the commoditization of fashion, it has nearly eliminated the appreciation for a well-dressed man, and instead, accepts a man who seems as though he just rolled out of bed, as long as it's the latest trend. I see men dressing with no purpose or direction nearly everywhere I look. Following this massive adoption of trend consumption for men, I wonder, are gentlemen lost altogether, or just rarer and farther between?

The Art of the Gentleman is sustained by etiquette, a code of discerning conduct, finesse in personal presentation, and to never miss an opportunity. It's about knowing how to walk into a room and own it. These are the same tenth century knight vows that I have been speaking of.

The Art of the Gentleman hinges upon making a first and lasting good impression. The Gentleman knows that his clothing is an investment in fabrics and craftsmanship that will last a lifetime. Furthermore, the Art of the Gentleman transcends fashion and reaches into morals, ethics and culture. This means being steeped in literature, rich in conversation, and an overall appreciation for the arts. It means having an appreciation for the finer things, not for how much they cost, but for the value they bring to one's life.

One of my favorite fashion icons, Karl Lagerfeld, once warned, "Sweatpants are a sign of defeat. You lost control of your life, so you bought some sweatpants." It seems our society has been caught wearing sweatpants. Cheapened by trends and quick fixes, we've lost sight of what fashion meant in the first place. Now, before I go on, let me be clear: I do own a pair of sweats. There is a time and a place for everything. For me, it's at home on a cold night by the fire while savoring a great bottle of wine. I will also gladly wear jeans, boots, and a suede jacket to a meeting at Soho House, but this isn't a chase for the loudest and trendiest items. Though I will participate in a trend here and there and wear a pair of sweats, I have not lost my sense of value for the craftsmanship and quality of even these items. Anyone can wear jeans and a T-shirt or sweatshirt. It takes a specific type of man, a "Gentleman," to put on a classic outfit with confidence. Even pairing and layering properly require a keen eye for detail. A true aficionado owns his style beyond what's "in fashion."

In this era of rampant trend cycles, of quality shifting to quantity, and standards for fabric integrity decreasing, true seekers of luxury and quality are left with few places to turn.

A recent study in a psychology journal states that men who dressed impeccably negotiated more profitable deals and did so with higher levels of testosterone. They were having more fun because they felt better about themselves, and more so because they knew it. There is a saying, "Dress for the life you want, not for the life you have." It's also safe to assume that this motto is true for both men and women. We are psychologically influenced by the clothing choices we make. If a woman wakes up in the morning, takes the time to care about how she dresses, she feels confident and she will carry the power of that choice throughout the entire day. That's why we need to laser in on the current shift in the market for apparel. I've noticed that with the rise of social media and blogging; specifically, men are caring more than ever about what they look like. It's fascinating to watch the rise of men's streetwear and see how luxury brands have adjusted and absorbed this anomaly. Rather than miss out on a rising trend in the market, many luxury groups have taken advantage, reinventing their collections to feed the craze of the moment.

This shift in the market leaves me wondering, with men's increased interest in fashion being directed towards casual streetwear, what will the next thirty years look like? Will men completely toss suits by the wayside? What will become of the Art of the Gentleman, and of the legacies of the titled knight and others such as Clark Gable, Humphrey Bogart, Fred Astaire, the Duke of Windsor, and even Frank Sinatra? With the rise in men's luxury streetwear, how can we steer the focus back towards dressing - and acting - like gentlemen? My prediction is that this cycle will eventually fade, and that refined menswear will have a resurgence. Fashion is always cyclical. While fads come and go, investing in a finely crafted and well-tailored garment will benefit you for a lifetime. I want us to be able to focus on the importance of craftsmanship in both products and philosophy. We can bring back style, poise, and the crucial importance of being a connoisseur. We can help redefine the attributes of what makes the modern and sophisticated man and ultimately return to the Art of the Gentleman.

There is a time and a place for everything, and it is up to us to live by a higher code. It is not exclusive to men; women too can live by this code. No matter how much money you have or what you wear, there is an elevated way to live your life that brings you what you want to attract. This is larger than our reputation and who we are, it extends to future generations.

Being a Gentleman Is an Intentional Way of Living

With a simple choice to live by a higher standard, we set the pace and tone for our life, our business relationships, and romantic relationships. Children, men and women – everyone around us is affected by how we do things, whether we realize it or not. I'll give you an example. Everyone who knows me, knows that I curse. I do in a few appropriate situations. I even went through an intentional process of editing this book to make sure that I could appeal to all audiences. I want young men and women to read this book and understand the code I represent. I do not want to limit myself and who my work is acceptable for. I believe in being as thoughtful in the way I dress, as I am in every area of my life. I mentioned this earlier: *How you do anything is how you do everything.*

I also find it important to instill this same code into my children. I take them to fine-dining experiences, like Spago and show them the importance of being properly dressed and showing respect at restaurants. I am teaching them how to wear a dress shirt and jacket; they get to learn how to properly put a napkin on their lap; they learn how to use flatware; they get to learn how to sit up straight and how to chew with their mouth closed. I am teaching them to be gentlemen and how to be kind. I am teaching them chivalry and the importance of being appreciative. It is also a balance. I love my children and do things for them, but I don't spoil them. While fancy dinners are not the norm, it has a purpose. It is also important to enjoy a burger from the local stand, working on a farm, as well as giving back to families in need and the community. These are important components that will teach them the importance of living a balanced life. It's all important to build confidence, humility, empathy for others, pride in accomplishment, and intention in relationships.

There are moments in our life that define us and give us clarity on our path. On my journey to creating Kingsway and the on-going quest for establishing my legacy, there have been moments in my life that made me realize that I wasn't in control. I say this because there could be no way on this earth that I could have orchestrated such extraordinary people and situations that all fit together like an intricate puzzle.

XXII. CREATING A LEGACY

By now, you've had an understanding of some of the things I've been through in my life, and how it's led me to where I am today. Many people will tell you that life happens to you; I believe it happens for you. There is nothing wrong with small or humble beginnings. It is something I have learned early. I know that it's not a dishonor to start small, but it is a dishonor not to try and maximize the gifts that God has bestowed on you. We must continuously strive to grow and be better. What are you doing this all for? What's your calling? What's your purpose? What's your legacy?

These are the questions that I have asked myself most of my life. When I built CCCXXXIII, my vision was simple. I wanted to make the best of the best, the same way I did when creating King of Clubs. For me, the creative experience begins with respecting and remembering the past while still being innovative. I don't believe in compromising quality or craftsmanship. I aimed to achieve a sense of classic, timeless products with deep inspiration from centuries ago. When we were building the brand, I knew from the start I wanted to get involved in ready-to-wear, shoes, fragrances, and other products, but I purposely decided to start with accessories.

Everything I do has to be thoughtful and intentional, with the maximum attention to detail. I have sometimes been described as being overly obsessive. So naturally when it came to our logo, I wanted something unique that had deep meaning. I commissioned Neil Bromley, a Heraldic and Medieval illuminator artist who lives in Devon, UK, and is a craft member of the Society of Heraldic Art, to create our calligraphic logo. We collaborated with each other to design something that was close to my heart and something that would have a deep sense of history. I wanted to tap into past centuries; it was pulling at my spirit. Neil is actually one of the last known medieval artists alive and has been commissioned multiple times by the Royal House of Windsor. In 2013, to celebrate Her Majesty, Queen Elizabeth's sixtieth year as a monarch, Bromley created an ornate royal family tree poster print, detailing the royal line of succession since 1066. Featuring elegant calligraphy and decorated with intricate heraldic artwork, the piece was originally designed and painted on vellum in twenty-three-carat gold, using the traditional techniques that have made Neil a specialist in his field.

The initial CCCXXXIII logo design was in gold, and after determining that this is what I wanted, we started to work on the crown imagery that would be an integral part of our trademark. We started the design and got through several versions featuring three distinct crosses, and I recall there was a point where I wanted a slight difference between the crosses. Neil strongly suggested against it because every crown possesses symmetrical features, which had been done that way for thousands of years. If you look at our logo today, the three crosses are slightly different; this was to stand for the Father, the Son, and the Holy Spirit. The design was a dream from God who inspired me to create the crown and the design of the original attaché. I remember waking up one morning and was late for a meeting. After a cup of coffee, I quickly jumped in the shower (I do a lot of my thinking in the there) and it hit me hard. I remembered my dream. It was God showing me what the bag looked like. I immediately grabbed the pencil and paper I have in my shower and started to draw the first concept of the attaché featuring the very distinctive three coins. It was this drawing I kept and used as a reference for the creation of the very first attaché. It also led to the creation of the custom hardware that you see on all of our products.

Faith is behind the creation of this entire company. Faith to dare and dream things only I could see. I am always inspired and driven by my beliefs. I have said many times; you shouldn't fake it to you make it, you should "Faith it till you make it." Faith is NOW, not the future. Faith is not a worldly emotion, it is a supernatural force, and the faster you learn this, I believe the quicker you will discover things deep down inside of you. I've relied on my faith through thick and thin; it has protected me throughout my life. I wasn't always a believer, and there's so much more to that story, which we will keep for another day. I even have a mustard seed necklace I wear at all times. It's a reminder of my faith and one of my favorite bible verses. Mathew 17:20, "I say to you, if you have faith as a mustard seed, you will say to this mountain, 'Move from here to there,' and it will move, and nothing will be impossible for you."[1] It has been through constant faith and belief in myself that has allowed me to do the impossible. Later in life, after creating this necklace for myself, I found out that my grandmother and her grandmother used to wear mustard seed necklaces. Coincidence? At this point in my life I don't think so.

A few years ago, I was doing some soul-searching and having many conversations with God. I was on a deep spiritual journey that tested my faith. I was shown parts of my life that affected me and that needed correcting. I gained so much wisdom from these times, which allowed me to forgive people from my past, gain clarity and ultimately led me to grow as a man.

I will never forget Father's Day, June 18, 2017, I went in my home gym in the garage to workout. I was on the treadmill listening to the album by Kim Walker-Smith, "Spirit Break Out" playing very loudly. I kept hearing this loud voice: "Will you be my king on earth?" I heard it about two or three times, the third time it was the loudest, to the point that I stopped the music and asked if somebody was there. With no answer, I turned the music back on thinking I was hearing things. It was 8:03 p.m., and I heard it again, and at that moment, I knew that it was from God. Repeating what He had said, "Will you be a king on earth?" My reply was, "Of course I will." Within a matter of seconds, right before my eyes, Jesus appeared, in a giant glowing presence. It was as if the whole room was lit up with unbelievable energy, it was startling. Before I could even react, as He stood at the base of the treadmill he said, "Now, you are ready, my son." He reached with both hands to his heart and pulled out a ball of light, which I presumed was a new heart and pushed it into my chest. It was like a strike of lightning hit me. I started to lose my balance. So, I hit the emergency button, and climbed down off the treadmill. It was intense. I shut off the music and walked right to my bed. I didn't turn off any lights and didn't even shower, despite the fact I was still sweaty from the workout. I simply couldn't do anything and just passed out. I woke up the next morning officially a changed man. It says in Ezekiel 36:26, "I will give you a new heart and put a new spirit within you; I will take the heart of stone out of your flesh and give you a heart of flesh."[2] I know I was given a new heart that night.

From that moment on, my entire existence as a human being, friend, father, businessman, leader, and mentor changed. Miracle after miracles have happened throughout my life and continue to happen. I pray boldly in addition to reading His word daily. God is at the center of everything I do, and He is always showing up in my life.

They say kings are held to a higher standard and it wasn't until October of 2019 that I would begin to understand more. It was a Sunday morning, and I was supposed to attend a high-profile event that evening. But God had a different plan. I got a text from my mother saying she found the King family reunion flyer from 1983. I've vaguely remembered attending that event and asked her to send me some images. As I'm looking at the crest on the very first page, I tell my mother on the phone how much this looks like the King family crest from England, the resemblance was almost identical, with a few minor changes. I could feel this overwhelming pull in my spirit to keep searching. She said to go to ancestry.com to take a deeper look into this. A year prior, I'd already done my DNA testing, and it was one-hundred percent European with a mix of forty percent British and Irish and thirty-three percent French and German.

I started to fill out some of the ancestry forms online going back-and-forth with my mother, who was at home going through birth certificates and sending me copies and images of grandparents. We were looking up names, verifying dates and this continued for hours. I started to feel a weird sense of purpose. I began to feel the presence of God again, I felt like I was going to get to finally discover my ancestors. I immediately sent a text around 2:00 p.m. canceling my plans for that evening; instead, I cleared my time to continue my search. It was hours and hours of research going as far back as the 1300s. I discovered even more. I came across my fourteenth great grandfather, Everard Digby, and the famous Gunpowder Plot of 1605.[3] I kept digging a little further and also discovered that Everard's Son was married to Mary Anne Cope, whose grandfather on her side was Sir William Cope, my fifteenth great grandfather. Sir William was the Conferrer to Henry VII, the King of England and Lord of Ireland. The Arms of Cope of Hanwell bare three roses and three fleurs-de-lys. Now fleurs-de-lys play an important part in my life, I'll share more on that in a few.

I started to get a headache. It was a lot to take in. Some people married several times, some had multiple children who subsequently had many offspring and others had as many as five or six children. It was a giant maze sprawled across my dining room table and on to the floor. I kept expanding and found members of the family attached to the House of Plantagenet, which would explain my French DNA results. The Plantagenet Kings were often forced to negotiate compromises such as Magna Carta. They were defeated in the fifteenth century in the Hundred Years War and later had a rivalry, which brought about the Wars of the Roses, a decade-long fight for the English succession. Henry VII became King of

England and ending the Wars of the Roses, giving rise to the Tudor Dynasty.

I kept digging and found out Edward III who was King of England was a distant relative as well (to be as accurate as possible, my connection to him goes back some twenty generations ago). He transformed the Kingdom of England into one of the most formidable military powers in Europe; to mark his claim to the French crown, his coat of arms showed three lions of England with the three fleurs-de-lys of France. I froze in my shoes. I have three fleurs-de-lys tattooed on my left arm and a lion tatted on my right arm. What was going on? The fleur-de-lys has been a guiding sign my whole life, countless times it has led me somewhere or acted as a confirmation even when I was younger and had no idea what it was or even how to pronounce it. It was even on the water I drink, Acqua Panna which birthplace was in the Medici Family villa in Tuscany. If you know me, I stock these glass bottles by the pallet at my house and have been for more than twelve years. I stare at the signature fleurs-de-lys logo every day. I mean, I have always been fascinated with the Medici Family. Was this the reason I was creating my brand in Italy first? The reason God showed up to me in Italy while standing in front of that family tree? The Renaissance period and medieval history were something that always fascinated me. I had always felt a deep connection to these periods. I have an affinity and attachment to the thirteenth century. What did this all mean? Was I being called all along? Why now?

Finally, I headed to bed and got some much-needed sleep. I ended up speaking to a close friend of mine, Nicole, the next morning, explaining the findings. She says to me, "You should talk to my friend Brooke, she looked up her ancestry, and King Edward III was also related to her." Without delay, a group text comes across my screen "Connecting you both. I wonder if you're cousins. I love that I have two royal friends!"

Now there are so many illegitimate lines, especially King Henry I, who according to *The New York Times*[4] sired twenty-two illegitimate children. So, who knows with absolute certitude about anything that reaches that far in the past? We agreed to meet and connected that afternoon. She was on a different software called Family Searches, so I was excited to find out if there were similar results. We began to fill my sections out. We got pretty far down the tree, and she said, "Now, hit this button in the app 'Relatives Around Me.'" We both start laughing as if the results would reveal anything, and then it happened. We both get a popup screen saying, "Your 11th cousin." We break out laughing and saying, "No way." We started to compare and find where the match was and discover that one of our common distant relatives was Samuel Chapin, known as "The Puritan." I was blown away, not only finding out that we were related, and that King Edward III was, in fact, a distant relative, but that "The Puritan" brought Christianity to America according to history. That there was a statue of him at the Met Gala in NYC, where I happened to be heading there the next day. (I ended up going and seeing it.) I knew God was up to something. There were even other family members discovered that were reverends; Reverend Peter Hobart was my tenth great-grand uncle. I felt like I was finding a purpose. Was my calling again being confirmed? All I cared about, all I longed for deep in my heart, was coming to the surface. But what did it all mean? I mean, in reality it means nothing in today's world. There is no pot of gold, heredity to a throne or a giant castle owed to me. But it did give me a feeling of purpose and clarity as to why I was doing this.

For me, it was clear. These ancient times inspire me to create. I have talked about painting earlier in this book; since that first painting, I have created over eighty works of art that I pile up in a storage unit; it's a release for me. It inspires me to play with colors, relieves stress, and lets my mind wander and have visions and daydreams while doing so. I get those same creative juices flowing from cooking. It's so satisfying to prepare a fancy meal made from scratch, it can be for friends and family gatherings, for my sons, or if I just cook for myself. I have come to enjoy experiences in my life. I enjoy the simple pleasures like rosemary from my garden or oranges and lemons from my trees.

What does all this have to do with legacy? Well for starters, it was about getting some answers. It was also about clarity and fulfilling my purpose. It was, most of all, trying to make sense of a past I barely knew. It gave a purpose to my visions, beliefs, and way of life. It was this pathway I needed to follow, not only to leave for my children but hopefully for the world. When you think of leaving your legacy, you begin to think about your death. What would people remember me by? It gives you a new perspective on life. It was the first time I started to think of leaving something for my children beyond possessions. I want for them to continue to be inspired and embark on their own journey and experience change as a result. They say that history always repeats itself. Was it time for this to happen? Was I the one supposed to stand up and lead us back to the honor and ethics, and yes, chivalry, of centuries ago?

Really, who knows. I do know that it made me consider how I conduct myself and how it will impact my sons, grandchildren, and future generations to come. Earlier in this book, I shared the story of being in Italy and looking at that family tree. I wanted something that I hoped would survive me. I knew that I wanted to build something that would last for generations.

Building a legacy is never about being better than anybody else, it's about leaving your mark, a certain mentality, and your beliefs. It is about doing it your way. I've learned throughout my life that so much of us are caught up in pleasing other people or doing something that we think might make everybody happy. There will be those who, upon reading this book, won't agree, will laugh, or even judge, but there will also be some who will be inspired or touched in ways other books haven't. As humans we are always looking for validation, perhaps from a spouse, a parent, or friend and with social media these days, even a stranger. It's difficult to build anything substantial until you do what makes you happy and fulfills your purpose. Only when you look deep down inside that, you will find your way. We all have incredible gifts. My belief is that when we discover those and start to understand our purpose and calling, then, and only then, will you have the ability to build a legacy.

For me, it is no longer about my successes or failures; it's about doing what I was born to do. This is the great discovery and it took me a lifetime of experiences to get to this point. I had to get through it in order to become the person I am destined to be. Now I get to follow the necessary steps and path on the way to build my legacy. My works of art, designs, way of thinking, people I inspire, and businesses I build, all of these pursuits will eventually define my legacy. I want to leave behind my unique mindset and my way of looking at the world, my vision, and my gifts, this is what it's all about.

It has been a piece of my awakening. Writing this book has been part of that process. Kingsway is a way of living. It's creating a life-style and legacy brand that will be worth living for. It's also worth leaving behind for as many people as you can. It's far more than a business or even this book. The idea of the Art of the Gentleman is timeless and will be around forever. It is about our manners, the way we act and, of course, the way we live. My part and my legacy will help play a role in this, to help carry this torch, to shine a light on what matters. It's chivalry, a mindset, a unique moral code. It's even the code of the knights; it is Kingsway.

NOTES

II. Get Your Head in the Game

1. Carol S. Dweck, *Mindset the New Psychology of Success* (New York: Ballantine Books, 2016).
2. T. Harv Eker, *Secrets of the Millionaire Mind: Think Rich to Get Rich* (London: Piatkus, 2005).
3. Paulo Coelho, The Alchemist (New York: HarperCollins Publishers., n.d.).
4. James 3:2 (NKJV).
5. James 1:19 (NKJV).

III. Your Past Doesn't Have to Be Your Future

1. Kirk Varnedoe, Jackson Pollock, and Pepe Karmel, Jackson Pollock (New York: The Museum of Modern Art, 1998).

IV. Embrace Change

1. Alan Deutschman, *Change or Die: The Three Keys to Change at Work and in Life* (New York: Harper, 2008).
2. Paul Arden, *It's Not How Good You Are, It's How Good You Want to Be* (London: Phaidon, 2003).

VI. Dress for Success

1. James Sherwood, *Bespoke, The Men's Style of Savile Row*, n.d).
2. Michael L. Slepian et al., "The Cognitive Consequences of Formal Clothing," Social Psychological and Personality Science 6, no. 6 (2015).

VII. Make Room for Opportunity

1. Gary Keller, Dave Jenks, and Jay Papasan, *The Millionaire Real Estate Investor: Anyone Can Do It--Not Everyone Will* (New York: McGraw-Hill, 2005).
2. Steve Berges, *The Complete Guide to Flipping Properties* (Hoboken, NJ: J. Wiley & Sons, 2008).
3. Peter Conti and David Finkel, *How to Create Multiple Streams of Income:*

Buying Homes in Nice Areas with Nothing Down (Lakewood, CO: Peter Conti & David Finkel, 1999).

XI. Don't Let Others Drain You Dry

1. Neil Somerville, *The Answers* (London: Element, 2004).
2. Proverbs 18:21 (NKJV).

XIII. The Art of Giving Back

1. Matthew 6:1-4 (NKJV).

XVI. Get the Right People in the Room and Magic will Happen

1. *Forbes* magazine, September 2014.
2. Wine Atlas of the World.
3. The Sommelier Journal, January 2012. Top Releases of 2011.
4. *Forbes* magazine. September 2014.

XX. Tell Your Truth

1. *Red Obsession* (FilmBuff).
2. Franck Demaury, "Christopher R. King Et Aston Martin, Rendre Exclusif Une Création Ultime," Forbes France, October 11, 2018, https://www.forbes.fr/luxe/ christopher-r-king-et-aston-martin-rendre-exclusif-une-creation-ultime/?cn-reloaded=1).

XXII. Creating a Legacy

1. Mathew 17:20 (NKJV).
2. Ezekiel 36:26 (NKJV).
3. History.com Editors, "Gunpowder Plot," History.com (A&E Television Networks, November 9, 2009), https://www.history.com/topics/british-history/ gunpowder-plot).
4. Bill Ryan, "The Royal Family Tree Sprouts Unofficial Limbs," The New York Times (The New York Times, January 3, 1993), https://www.nytimes.com/ 1993/01/03/nyregion/the-royal-family-tree-sprouts-unofficial-limbs.html).

ACKNOWLEDGMENTS

None of this would have been possible without God. The constant encouragement of my close friend Rob Dyrdek pushed me to find my truth and put it on these pages. I had shelved the book for so many years, and he pressed me to put it out after reading an old copy.

I am indebted to so many people, too many to name you all. To everyone who have contributed stories and events in this book, I appreciate you for allowing me to tell the stories. There are so many memories, so many that didn't make the book, and so many more to create. Thank you to everyone who contributed by being interviewed and was so kind to lend their time for this process.

Thank you to everyone who helped me write this book: Kenny Kemp, who flew back and forth from Scotland and spent countless hours listening to my stories. Christine Andreu and Yves Le Sieur for your proofreading, editing, late night texts, and calls to help this high school dropout perfect this book. So... the responsibility for any mistakes or typographical errors that found their way into the finished book falls on your shoulders. I am of course kidding (well kind of). I appreciate you deeply. David Schwartz, for the design and layout of the cover and back cover, another project completed together. Meeno Peluce for the amazing photograph we captured in Milan to make the cover. He also shot the back cover (he kind of shoots everything). To Paul and Jessica for your help in the formatting of my ebook and helping with Amazon. To my soul sisters Nicole and Jaymee for your constant support and prayers.

Writing this book has been a journey and one of the hardest and rewarding accomplishments of my life.

A heartfelt thank you to my family who raised me with love and toughness, and to the two young men whom I have the privilege to call my sons, Zachary and Cruz. I'm already so proud of you, thank you for being my biggest source of motivation. I love you unconditionally.

ABOUT THE AUTHOR

Christopher R. King was raised by a single mother, dropped out of school in the tenth grade, and went on to build a real estate empire all before age twenty-six. After losing everything in the 2008 financial crash, his never-quit mindset built back his second fortune. He co-founded King of Clubs, an ultra-premium wine with Napa Valley legend, Robert Mondavi Jr., which they sold in 2017.

He is the founder and creative director of Christopher King / CCCXXXIII the luxury Italian-made leather goods company which is appreciated by an international list of discerning clients, including A-list celebrities, actors, musicians, and professional athletes. He also curated an exclusive one-of-a-kind 2018 DBS Superleggera, limited to only three, in collaboration with famed British automaker, Aston Martin.

A true believer in the Art of the Gentleman, King is on a mission to implement his "manners make society" mindset. He is on a quest to exemplify that chivalry is not dead. King currently spends his time between Beverly Hills and Milan. He is the proud father of two boys, Zachary and Cruz.

Made in the USA
San Bernardino, CA
12 May 2020